ELECTION AND REPROBATION

ELECTION AND REPROBATION

by

JAMES HENLY THORNWELL

WIPF & STOCK · Eugene, Oregon

Wipf and Stock Publishers
199 W 8th Ave, Suite 3
Eugene, OR 97401

Election and Reprobation
By Thornwell, James Henly
ISBN 13: 978-1-60608-031-3
Publication date 7/10/2008
Previously published by Baker Book House, 1961

ELECTION AND REPROBATION.

WHATSOEVER the Scriptures contain was designed by the Holy Spirit for our careful study and devout meditation, and we are required to search them habitually and prayerfully, since they contain the "words of eternal life." The doctrines of the Bible cannot prove hurtful unless they are perverted by ignorance or wrested by abuse. In examining, however, the more mysterious features of revealed truth, there are two extremes widely different, but perhaps equally dangerous, into which there is hazard of running—presumptuous curiosity on the one hand, and squeamish timidity on the other. Men of inquisitive and speculative minds are apt to forget that there are limits set to human investigation and research, beyond which it is impossible to pass with safety or satisfaction. To intrude with confidence into the unrevealed secrets of God's wisdom and purpose manifests an arrogance and haughtiness of intellect which cannot fail to incur the marked disapprobation of Heaven, and should always meet the prompt reprobation of the pious. Whatsoever is useful to be known God has kindly and graciously revealed, and it argues no less ingratitude than presumption to attempt to be "wise above what is written." Theology has already suffered greatly from the pride of human intellect. Men, anxious to know more than God has thought proper to communicate, or secretly dissatisfied with the form in which statements of Divine truth are made in the Bible, have recurred to philosophy and science to improve or to explain the doctrines of revelation. Sometimes the Scriptures stop too short, and then metaphysics and logic must be called in to trace their disclosures to the secret recesses of the Eternal mind. Sometimes the Scriptures and philosophy, " falsely so ·called," come into collision, and then the former must go through an exegetical transformation, so as to wear the shape which the latter would impress on them. All this is a wide departure from that simplicity of faith with which the Word of God should always be received. " All Scripture is given by inspiration of God," and to quarrel with it, or to attempt to push our investigations beyond it, is just to quarrel with the wisdom and goodness of the Deity Himself. It is tacitly charging the Holy Spirit with keeping back from men what it is important to their happiness to know. A deep conviction of the fullness and sufficiency of the Scriptures, combined with a hearty regard for their disclosures, is the only effectual check to this presumptuous pride. of intellect.

But while some thus madly attempt to overleap the boundaries which God has set to their knowledge, others, through excessive caution, are afraid to know what the Lord has actually revealed. This squeamish timidity is no less dishonouring to God, as it supposes that He has communicated some truths, in a moment of unlucky forgetfulness, which it would have been better to conceal, and flatly and palpably contradicts the assertion of Paul that all Scripture is " profitable." If we suffer ourselves to be deterred from a fearless exposition of Divine truth by the cavils and perversions of profane minds, we may just surrender all that constitutes the Gospel a peculiar system, and make up our minds to be content with the flimsy disclosures of Deism or the cheerless darkness of Atheism. The doctrines of the Trinity, of the incarnation of the Son, of the covenants, of imputation, etc., are all made the scoff of the impudent and the jest of the vain. Paul's doctrines were perverted to unholy purposes by the false apostles, but all their defamation and reproach could not make Paul ashamed of the truth, nor afraid to preach it. "One hoof of Divine truth," says the venerable Erskine, "is not to be kept back, though a whole reprobate world should break their necks on it." "The Scripture," says Calvin, "is the school of the Holy Spirit, in which, as nothing useful or necessary to be known is omitted, so nothing is taught which it is not beneficial to know." While, then, a presumptuous curiosity, on the one hand, may not be allowed to carry us beyond the Scriptures, let not a sickly timidity, on the other, induce us to fall below them. "Let the Christian man," as Calvin again says, "open his heart and his ears to all the discourses addressed to him by God, only with this moderation, that as soon as the Lord closes His sacred mouth he also shall desist from further inquiry. This will be the best barrier of sobriety, if in learning we not only follow the leadings of God, but as soon as He ceases to teach we give up our desire of learning. It is a celebrated observation of Solomon, 'that it is the glory of God to conceal a thing.' But as both piety and common sense suggest that this is not to be understood generally of everything, we must seek for the proper distinction, lest we content ourselves with brutish ignorance under the pretext of modesty and sobriety. Now, this distinction is clearly expressed in a few words by Moses: 'The secret things belong unto the Lord our God, but those things which are revealed belong unto us and to our children, that we may do all the words of this law.' Deut. xxix. 29. For we see how he enforces on the people attention to the doctrine of the law, only by the celestial decree, because it pleased God to promulgate it; and restrains the same people within those limits with this single reason, that it is not lawful for mortals to intrude into the secrets of God."

These preliminary remarks will not be taken amiss by any who are even tolerably acquainted with the state of opinion in the theological world on the great doctrine of predestination. Instead of attending to the Scriptures as a rule of infallible truth, and receiving the instructions derived from them with implicit faith, we find some men boldly scrutinizing those secrets of infinite wisdom which God has concealed in Himself; while others of less adventurous dispositions seem to be filled with apprehension lest the Holy Spirit has spoken indiscreetly and inculcated absolutely what should be received only with cautions and limitations. We readily assent to the proposition in words, but the unsanctified heart makes no small opposition to it, that the Word of God is truth, and that we are bound to receive all that it contains on the authority of its Author, independently of all other considerations. We are neither to question nor to doubt, but simply to interpret and believe. Philosophy and prejudice and everything else are to yield to the voice of God speaking in His Word. It is owing to a neglect of this simple but obvious principle that views so contradictory have been held and published of the doctrine of predestination, and the necessary consequence of such inconsistency of opinion has been to involve the discussion of the subject in no little difficulty and perplexity. In maintaining the true doctrines of the Bible, as set forth in orthodox standards, we have not only to encounter the violent, unmitigated opposition of Pelagians and Arminians, but the no less unwarrantable excesses of the Supralapsarians and Hopkinsians. While the former explain the decrees of God in such a way as to amount to a downright denial of their certainty and sovereignty, the latter have pushed their inquiries with a censurable boldness into the hidden things which belong only to the Lord, and in their explanations of what is actually revealed have departed widely from the simplicity of the Bible. The Westminster Confession of Faith has happily avoided both these extremes of squeamish timidity and presumptuous boldness, and has exhibited, with its usual clearness and precision, the true doctrine of the Scriptures. The limits of a single tract will not allow me to enter into the broad and extensive field of the Divine decrees generally, and therefore I shall confine myself to the single feature of this great subject presented in the inseparable doctrines of Election and Reprobation. The fixing of the eternal destiny of men and angels is but a single link in the golden chain of "God's eternal purpose, by which, according to the counsel of His own will, He freely and unchangeably ordains whatsoever comes to pass." In the discussion of this subject I shall first endeavour to state clearly what the doctrines of Election and Reprobation are, as set forth in the Standards of the Presbyterian Church. I shall next attempt to vindicate these doctrines by a candid reference to the Word of God. I shall, in the third place, refute the cavils of those who reject them, and conclude the whole with a few practical inferences.

I. From the account given in the third chapter of the Confession of Faith we deduce the following propositions, which will be recognized at once as a correct statement of orthodox views: 1. Election is personal. "By the decree of God, for the manifestation of His glory, some *men* and angels are predestinated unto everlasting life, and others foreordained to everlasting death. These men and angels thus predestinated and foreordained are *particularly* and *unchangeably* designed, and their number is so *certain* and *definite* that it cannot be either increased or diminished." Sec. 3, 4. Hence, it is not an election of nations and communities to external privileges, but of men "particularly and unchangeably designed," and that to everlasting life, as we shall soon see more fully. 2. Man, in the decree of Election, is regarded as a *fallen* being. "Wherefore, they who are elected, *being fallen in Adam,* are redeemed by Christ," etc. Sec. 6. That this is the settled opinion of the orthodox will appear yet more clearly from the decision of the Synod of Dort on this very point: "Election is the unchangeable purpose of God by which, before the foundation of the world, He did from the whole human race, *fallen by their own fault from original righteousness* into a state of sin and misery, elect to salvation in Christ, according to the good pleasure of His own will, out of His mere free grace, a certain number of individuals, neither better than others nor more worthy of His favour, but involved with others in a common ruin."[1] This was likewise the opinion of Calvin and Turrettin and the leading divines of the Secession Church of Scotland, such as the Erskines and Fisher and Boston. 3. It is an election to *everlasting life*, and includes all the means which the Scriptures lay down for accomplishing this glorious end. " As God has appointed the elect unto glory, so hath He, by the eternal and most free purpose of His will, foreordained all the means thereunto. Wherefore, they who are elected, being fallen in Adam, are redeemed by Christ; are effectually called unto faith in Christ by His Spirit working in due season; are justified, adopted, sanctified, and kept by His power through faith unto salvation." Sec. 6. 4. This election of individuals of Adam's fallen race to everlasting life was made from *eternity*. In proof of this there needs no appeal to any particular portion of the chapter, for it is either definitely stated or clearly implied from the first section to the last. 5. It is absolute or wholly irrespective of works, having no other originating or impulsive cause than the mere good pleasure of God's will. " Those of mankind that are predestinated unto life, God, before the foundation of the world was laid, according to His eternal and immutable purpose, and the secret counsel and good pleasure of His will, hath chosen in Christ, unto everlasting glory, out of His mere free grace and love, without any foresight of faith or good works, or perseverance in either of them, or any other thing in the creature, as conditions or causes moving Him thereunto; and all to the praise of His glorious grace." Sec. 5. In regard to Reprobation, the Confession teaches the following particulars: 1. The individuals reprobated are guilty and polluted, " being by nature the children of wrath." This follows from the fact that the reprobate, equally with the elect, " are fallen in Adam;" and in Section 7th, God is said to " pass by and to ordain them to dishonour and wrath

[1] Article vii.

for their sin." 2. God passes them by or refuses to elect them, and leaves them in that state of misery and ruin into which, by their own fault, they had plunged themselves. 3. He dooms them to the deserved punishment of their sins in the world to come by a righteous act of vindicatory justice. 4. In the decree of reprobation God acts absolutely. He passes by one and elects another only from His own good pleasure; but in inflicting and pronouncing the sentence of death, He acts as a righteous Judge in consigning the wicked to deserved punishment. In other words, none but a sinner can be a suitable subject of reprobation, and men are reprobated only as sinners; but one man is passed by and another elected, not because one was a greater sinner than the other, but because God saw fit to do so. All these points are embraced in Section 7. "The rest of mankind God was pleased, according to the unsearchable counsel of His own will, whereby He extendeth or withholdeth mercy as He pleaseth, for the glory of His sovereign power over His creatures, to pass by, and to ordain them to dishonour and wrath for their sin, to the praise of His glorious justice."

Of this tremendous doctrine, therefore, which has been the prolific subject of so much vituperation and abuse—which has supplied a theme of ranting declamation to many a stripling theologian, who, when all other subjects failed him, could fill out his allotted time and entertain his hearers by running a tilt against Calvin's ghost—which has made the knees of many a strong man shake and blanched the cheek of many an ignorant zealot with terror,—of this tremendous, this "horrible" doctrine, which has been represented as so revolting to every thing like reason, Scripture or common sense, this then is the sum: Man, having by wilful and deliberate transgression sinned against God, justly fell under His wrath and curse. All men, regularly descended from Adam, became "children of wrath, alienated from the life of God," and utterly destitute of original righteousness. The consequence was that sentence of condemnation actually passed upon all men. Unless we are prepared to question or impugn the stainless justice of God, we must admit that this sentence, thus solemnly passed upon the race, was a *righteous* sentence. Out of this race of guilty and polluted sinners, thus justly condemned, God graciously and eternally elected some to life and happiness and glory, while He left the rest in their state of wretchedness and ruin, and determined to inflict upon them the punishment which they justly deserved. The reason why He elected some and passed by others, when all were equally undeserving, is to be referred wholly to Himself—to the counsel of His own will or to His mere good pleasure.

I have been thus particular in deducing a plain statement of this doctrine from the Standards of the Church, because it is so difficult to meet with any fair or consistent account of it from writers who oppose it. They indulge too freely in the merest caricatures, or deduce their whole views from dislocated and disjointed expressions of Calvinistic divines. It would be no hard matter to show, by quotations from Calvin and Turrettin and the published Confessions of the Reformed Churches, that the statement just given is a fair exposition of the views which have usually been regarded as orthodox from the period of the Reformation until now. That there have been men who have overleaped the bounds of sobriety and modesty, and have consequently lost themselves in the mists of Supralapsarian and Hopkinsian error, need not and will not be denied ; but then their excesses are no more to be regarded as the genuine doctrines of Calvinistic churches than the wild speculations of Clarke on the Sonship of Christ and the omniscience of God as the genuine doctrines of the Wesleyan Methodists. In ascertaining the doctrines of a Church, we must appeal to her standards ; and having done so in this instance, and given, in the words of the Confession, the precise position of the Presbyterian Church, I proceed to show that her views are scriptural.

II. Widely as men may differ in their views of predestination, it is generally conceded by all who profess any reverence for the Word of God that there is an election, of some sort, to eternal life made known in the Scriptures. But there is much violent and bitter opposition to that account of it which places a crown of absolute sovereignty on the head of Jehovah, and prostrates man in entire dependence upon His will. In deducing the scriptural argument, I shall endeavour to arrange the texts under the several heads, or rather upon the separate points, made out in the explanation or statement of the doctrine from the Confession of Faith.

1. First, then, election is *personal;* that is, it is a choice of *individuals,* from the corrupt mass of our fallen race, to everlasting life. I am far from intending to insinuate that in every instance in which words expressive of election are used in the Scriptures a personal election to eternal life must of course be understood. On the contrary, it is freely admitted that the Scriptures speak of the choice of nations to peculiar privileges, of the choice of individuals to particular offices, and of the choice of Christ to the mediatorial work. All this is fully conceded, but yet there are passages which cannot, without unwarrantable violence, be interpreted in any other way than as teaching the doctrine of personal election to eternal life. " According as He hath chosen us in Him before the foundation of the world, that we should be holy and without blame before Him in love." Eph. i. 4. Here election is expressly said to be personal—" *hath chosen us,*" that is, Paul himself and the Christians at Ephesus. The epistle is directed to " the saints which are at Ephesus, and the faithful in Christ Jesus." i. 1. Here then is not an election of nations or communities to external privileges, but an election of individuals to everlasting life. In verses 5, 6, 7, 11 we have a more particular view of the blessing which they received in consequence of their election, and which cannot, by any ingenuity of criticism, be plausibly distorted into national advantages. " Having predestinated us unto the adoption of children by Jesus Christ, to Himself," etc. ; and again, " In whom we have redemption through His blood, the forgiveness of sins, according to the

riches of His grace." Those, therefore, to whom Paul was writing were "saints, faithful in Christ Jesus, adopted to be sons, redeemed and forgiven," and all these privileges he traced to the election of which he was speaking. Are there any so blind as not to see that these are saving blessings, and that those who were addressed as possessing them were *individuals* and not communities or nations? But it has been said that Paul could not know that the whole Church at Ephesus were elect. To this it may be readily replied that Paul does not say so. He sufficiently designates the individuals of whom he was speaking by the characteristics noticed above. Macknight, always anxious to fritter away the peculiar features of the Gospel, tells us in his note on the fourth verse that the election here spoken of is "that election which before the foundation of the world God made of holy persons of all nations to be His children and people, and to enjoy the blessing promised to such." Upon this singular note it is enough for my present purpose to remark—(1.) That it sufficiently admits the fact that the election here spoken of is personal. But (2.) that it was not, however, an election of "holy persons," but an election to be holy, "that we might be holy and without blame before Him in love." (3.) That these Ephesians, previously to their acceptance of the Gospel, were "dead in trespasses and sins, walked according to the prince of the power of the air, the spirit that now worketh in the children of disobedience," etc. ii. 1–3. They could not possibly, therefore, have been elected as "holy persons," seeing that they were utterly destitute of all pretensions to holiness.

I might here refer to the cases of Ishmael and Isaac and of Esau and Jacob adduced by the Apostle in the ninth chapter of Romans as examples, respectively, of personal election and righteous reprobation. These cases are conclusive on the point. The attempts of Socinian and Arminian writers to pervert that celebrated chapter from its natural and obvious meaning will be considered sufficiently in another part of this discussion.

2. The second point to be proved is, that man in the decree of election was regarded as a *fallen being.* Three opinions have been maintained by divines as to the light in which he was looked upon in this decree. The first is that of the Supralapsarians; the second, that of our Standards; and the third, that of the Arminians and Remonstrants at the Synod of Dort. The Supralapsarians take their name from the fact that in the decree of election and reprobation they suppose that God regarded man not even as yet created, or only as created and not as fallen. They, consequently, look upon the creation and fall as only intermediate steps through which man was to pass in accomplishing this great decree. To this scheme there are insuperable objections— (1.) The very ideas of election and reprobation suppose man to be involved already in a state of sin and misery. While in a state of holiness in their covenant head all men were regarded as equally righteous, and equally shared in their Maker's approbation. The fall, therefore, must take place before such a distinction could be made as this doctrine supposes; I mean that God in the counsels of eternity must have looked upon man as lost and ruined, since otherwise a determination to save some, and to leave others in their wretchedness and ruin, could not be expressed without a " solecism in language," and much less " conceived without confusion of thought." The very idea of salvation implies misery, and a determination to save implies a view or knowledge of that misery. It is plain, then, that sin and misery, in the individuals elected and reprobated, is an indispensable prerequisite. It might be objected here that in the case of the angels who stood election did not suppose a fall; but I would answer that the cases are not parallel. It was not a decree to save the angels from sin, but from sinning, and therefore they could be regarded only as liable to fall. But in the case immediately before us there is a decree to save men from a state of guilt and ruin, and

yet they are not involved in guilt and ruin! (2.) If it be maintained that man is not even regarded as created, we are thrown into still more perplexing absurdity. It is hard to conceive how a being not yet created can become the subject of such a decree at all. The decree of creation must be first in order of nature, or election and reprobation will be concerned not about men, but nonentities. (3.) What is said of this doctrine in the Scriptures is usually referred to the mercy and justice of God. The elect are monuments erected to the "praise of the glory of His grace," and the reprobate are "vessels of wrath," or of righteous and just displeasure; but how this could be said when man had not yet become obnoxious to God's justice, nor had yet been in a situation of wretchedness to require His mercy, it is hard to conceive. Sin is that alone which renders man a proper object of reprobation, and misery is the proper object of mercy. For these reasons—and many others might be adduced—I am led to regard the Supralapsarian scheme as untenable and false. The whole current of Scripture testimony is in favour of the doctrine of our Standards, commonly called Sublapsarianism. "I have chosen you out of the world, therefore the world hateth you." John xv. 19. The elect here are the objects of the Divine choice while belonging to the world, and the world means corrupt and fallen man, as is plain from its hating the righteous and godly. We are said to be "chosen in Christ"—that is, to be redeemed and saved by Him—which implies that when chosen we are guilty and polluted. Again: "Hath not the potter power over the clay, of the same lump to make one vessel unto honour and another unto dishonour?" Rom. ix. 21. That the lump here represents corrupt and ruined human nature is plain from the following considerations which I translate from Turrettin: " 1. It is the lump from which vessels of mercy and wrath are formed—one for honour, the other for dishonour, but wrath and mercy necessarily suppose sin and misery. 2. It is the same lump from which Isaac and Ishmael, Jacob and Esau are taken, who are brought forward, respectively, as examples of gratuitous election and of righteous and free reprobation. This must be the corrupt mass of human nature, because the Apostle speaks of Jacob and Esau as twins conceived in the womb, and therefore as sinners." It is no valid objection that the children are represented as having done neither good nor evil, for this is manifestly to be understood comparatively. Jacob had done no good and Esau no evil which caused the one to be preferred and the other rejected. It was not Jacob's being better than Esau, nor Esau's being worse than Jacob, which induced God to elect the one and reject the other.

The "vessels of wrath" (Rom. ix. 23) are represented as being "fitted for destruction" during the time that God bears with them in great patience and long-suffering, which seems to be inconsistent with the idea that they could have been "vessels of wrath" before they yet became "fitted for destruction" by sin and depravity. But, probably, the most pointed and remarkable passage on this subject is Ezek. xvi. 6: "But when I passed by thee, and saw thee polluted in thine own blood, I said unto thee when thou wast in thy blood, Live; yea, I said unto thee when thou wast in thy blood, Live." Here the elect, of whom Jerusalem was a symbol, are represented by the figure of a filthy and outcast infant, finding from none either sympathy or aid, but so loathsome in its person as to be abandoned in the "open field" the very day on which it was born. Verses 4, 5. The Lord represents Himself as looking upon this wretched infant thus polluted in its blood with an eye of compassion, and commanding it to "live." Ver. 6. Effectual calling cannot be intended by the word "live" here, because in effectual calling the soul is married to Christ, but in this passage the elect are represented as not yet of a marriageable age. Therefore the word must denote only God's *purpose to save*, and the passage thus interpreted shows conclusively in what light the elect are regarded in the decree of election. This interpretation will probably be confirmed by considering this verse in connection with the two following. In verse 7, God describes the growth of this miserable infant until it became a marriageable woman. "I have caused thee to multiply as the bud of the field; thou hast increased and waxen great, and thou art come to excellent ornaments; thy breasts are fashioned, and thine hair is grown, whereas thou wast naked and bare." The infant, having thus become a young woman and of marriageable age, the marriage or the union of the elect with Christ in effectual calling is celebrated in verse 8: "Now when I passed by thee, and looked upon thee, behold thy time was the time of love, and I spread my skirt over thee, and covered thy nakedness; yea, I sware unto thee, and entered into a covenant with thee, saith the Lord God, and thou becamest mine." Here, then, we have much the same view of the inseparable connection between election and vocation which Paul gives us in the 8th of Romans, and here it is clearly demonstrated that men are elected in that state from which they are called, which is a state of sin, condemnation and misery. The views of the Arminians, who suppose that man is regarded as believing or unbelieving in the decree of election and reprobation, will be refuted in another part of this discussion.

3. It is an election to *everlasting life or salvation*. "But we are bound to give thanks always to God for you, brethren, beloved of the Lord, because God hath from the beginning chosen you to salvation through sanctification of the Spirit and belief of the truth." 2 Thess. ii. 13. "For God hath not appointed us to wrath, but to obtain salvation by our Lord Jesus Christ." 1 Thess. v. 9. In both these texts the word *salvation* is probably used in reference to the state of glory beyond the grave. The first text is peculiarly forcible. The Apostle had been giving a graphic and appalling account of the revelation of the "man of sin," through whose seductive influence many souls would be led to reject the truth and be given over to judicial blindness, and finally be damned. Such statements as these were well calculated to

alarm the faithful, especially weak believers. The Apostle therefore shows in the text cited that there is no ground of apprehension to the real children of God; they are chosen to salvation, and therefore cannot come short of it. In order that the Thessalonian Christians might be able to receive the comfort of this truth, that the elect are absolutely safe, he points out the marks of election or the evidences of it—" sanctification of the Spirit and belief of the truth." The second text is equally clear. The Apostle is exhorting the Thessalonians to a diligent discharge of Christian duty. He had urged the unexpectedness of the Lord's coming as one motive, and presents another in the text I have quoted, and that is the certainty of success. The Lord has destined us to salvation; we can therefore discharge our Christian duties in confidence and hope. The election of God is a sufficient security against disappointment. The word salvation, however, is not always used in this sense when applied to the elect. In fact, it is a word of extensive signification, including in the language of Scripture what we commonly mean by grace and glory. Many of the absurd consequences which have been rashly and intemperately charged upon the doctrine of election would vanish at once before a correct apprehension of the true nature of eternal life. It is a common but erroneous opinion that the happiness of heaven is that alone which the Scriptures designate by this phrase, and those who entertain this error generally have crude conceptions of what constitutes the blessedness of glory. A slight acquaintance with the Bible, however, will show us that all believers even in this world are in actual and irreversible possession of eternal life. " My sheep hear my voice, and I know them, and I give unto them *eternal life*." " He that hath the Son hath *life*." That life which is implanted in the soul in regeneration, which is developed in sanctification and completed in glory, is what the Scriptures call eternal life, and it is called eternal because by the grace of God it is absolutely imperishable. There are not wanting passages of Scripture in which the word *life* is used in its full latitude of meaning: "I am the living bread which came down from heaven; if any man eat of this bread he *shall live for ever.*" John vi. 51, 57.

The scriptural meaning of *salvation* is deliverance from the curse, power and love of sin. The word in general implies deliverance from evil, but it is always, in the Bible, positive as well as negative, and imports the bestowment of a corresponding good. The blind, when healed by our Saviour, are said to be saved—that is, they are delivered from the evil of blindness, and receive the corresponding blessing of sight. So sinners are said to be saved by Christ, because through "the faith of Him" they are delivered from the evils of their natural state, and receive the blessings of a gracious state. Were it possible that a man who had obtained the forgiveness of sin should afterward fail of the blessedness of heaven, there is no assignable sense in which it could be said that he was saved. If there be any difference in the spiritual import of the words *salvation* and *life*, it would seem to be this, that the former has a more pointed reference to the evils from which we are delivered by grace, and the latter to the benefits of which we become partakers. It is true that these words are not always used in their fullest latitude, but are sometimes confined to one and sometimes to another feature of the general meaning. This, however, is a strong proof of the inseparable connection between grace and glory. In accordance with these remarks it may be observed—(1.) That salvation implies pardon and gratuitous acceptance. Luke i. 77: "To give knowledge of salvation unto His people by the remission of their sins." The original is, "in the remission of their sins"—that is, when our sins are pardoned we become partakers of salvation. Luke xix. 9: "This day is salvation come to this house." Whatever else the word may mean here, pardon of sin must be one of the blessings which Jesus conferred on Zacchæus. The curse of the law is what the

Scriptures mean by the " wrath to come," and no one can doubt that deliverance from this forms an important element of salvation. But we are delivered from the curse and covenant claims of the law in our gratuitous justification and pardon. (2.) Salvation implies regeneration and progressive sanctification, or the production and development of the new nature. Titus iii. 5: " Not by works of righteousness which we have done, but according to His mercy, He saved us by the washing of regeneration and the renewing of the Holy Ghost." Here the washing or cleansing of regeneration, which is explained to be the renewing of the Holy Ghost, is in so many words stated to be an element of salvation. Jesus received His name by the express and solemn appointment of God, because He should " save His people from their sins." The spiritual life which the Holy Spirit communicates in regeneration, and fosters and strengthens in sanctification, is of the same nature, though different in degree and the circumstances of its exercise, with the life of glory at God's right hand. The one is represented as an earnest of the other, and an earnest must be of the same kind with that of which it is an earnest. If, then, eternal blessedness is a part of our salvation, the new nature here necessarily must be. All, therefore, who are elected to salvation are elected to sanctification in the full scriptural extent of that word. Hence, the Apostle says that we are chosen, " that we might be holy and without blame before Him in love." Eph. i. 4. Hence, the Thessalonians are said to be " chosen to salvation through sanctification of the Spirit and belief of the truth ;" and hence, it is said, " We are His workmanship, created in Christ Jesus unto good works, which God hath before ordained that we should walk in them." Eph. ii. 10. (3.) Salvation implies the blessedness of heaven. This is such a common and familiar use of the term that we need not waste time in adducing texts.

From this short examination of the scriptural meaning of two words in very common use, we have seen that the

Standards of the Church have adhered closely to the Word of God in resolving election to salvation into election to all the privileges of redemption in this world as well as the world to come. Salvation is one great whole, and wherever it begins to exist it takes hold upon eternity. The blessedness of heaven is the result of election; so is personal holiness on earth—the grand preparative for glory; so is faith in the Lord Jesus—the great shield by which sin and Satan are effectually subdued. It would be a monstrous conception to suppose that men were elected to salvation, and yet not elected to a certain employment of the means by which alone salvation is secured. The Scriptures show conclusively—(1.) That effectual calling is the fruit of election. 2 Tim. i. 9: "Who hath saved us, and *called* us with an holy calling, not according to our works, but according to His own purpose and grace, which was given us in Christ Jesus before the world began." Rom. viii. 30: "Moreover, whom He did predestinate them He also called." (2.) As a matter of course, faith is the fruit of election. Eph. ii. 8: It is called the "gift of God." Phil. i. 29: "Unto you it is *given* to believe on Christ." Col. ii. 12: "Buried with Him in baptism, wherein also ye are risen with Him through the faith of the operation of God who hath raised Him from the dead." Heb. xii. 2: Jesus is regarded as "the Author and Finisher of our faith." 1 Cor. xii. 9: "To another, faith by the same Spirit," and saving faith is spoken of distinctively as the faith of "God's elect." (3.) But perhaps the most conclusive scriptural authority that all the blessings of redemption are included in election to eternal life is to be found in Romans viii. 29, 30: "For whom He did foreknow He also did predestinate to be conformed to the image of His Son, that he might be the firstborn among many brethren. Moreover, whom He did predestinate, them He also called, and whom He called, them He also justified, and whom He justified, them He also glorified." In these verses we have—1st, the election of God or His determination to save a chosen number: "Whom

He did foreknow." The connection of this verse with the preceding, and of this clause with the succeeding, sufficiently determines the meaning of the word "foreknow." Those who are said to be called in verse 29 are called according to God's "purpose," and in this verse their calling is coupled with God's foreknowledge. To foreknow, therefore, is to purpose or determine, or, what in this connection is just the same, to choose. This is a common and familiar meaning of the word. Rom. ii. 2; 1 Pet. i. 20. 2dly. We have the purpose of God to render them holy: "He also did predestinate to be conformed to the image of His Son," etc. Those whom He elected He determined to sanctify, to make holy even as Christ was holy. 3dly. We have the steps of the actual accomplishment of this decree: "Whom He did predestinate, them He also called;" that is, by the word of the Gospel, and the efficacious operation of the Spirit, He brings them into saving union with Christ, that so they may be conformed to His image. This is the common and familiar acceptation of the word in the writings of Paul. 1 Cor. i. 9, 24, etc. 4thly. We have the justification and final and complete salvation of those who were foreknown: "Whom He called, them He also justified, and whom He justified, them He also glorified." Being united to Christ in their effectual calling, they become partakers of His righteousness and grace, by which their justification, sanctification and glorification are infallibly secured. From this celebrated passage we see that "election, calling, justification and salvation are indissolubly united."

4. Election to everlasting life or salvation is *eternal*. Whatsoever purposes God now has, or ever will have, in regard to the destiny of men, He always has had. It would be a serious and dangerous detraction from the glory of the Divine unchangeableness to suppose that exigencies can arise in the government of the world calling for a change of the Divine purposes, or for a new and unexpected course of Providence. "Known unto God are all His works from the beginning of the world." Acts xv. 18. His all-seeing

eye brings all possible events within the light of a present and infallible omniscience. What He is now He was from all eternity, and will continue to be the same everlastingly. Succession of time can only be applied to Him in accommodation to our weak capacities, since all things past and future are "naked and opened to the eyes of Him with whom we have to do." But while, owing to the simplicity and eternity of the Divine nature, there cannot be conceived in God a succession of time, nor consequently various and successive decrees, yet we may justly speak of His decrees as prior or posterior in point of nature. Though they all constitute but one eternal act of the Divine will, the objects about which they are concerned are connected with each other by various relations, and the decrees themselves may be spoken of in a language accommodated to these diversified relations. In ordinary life we often see effects and causes coexistent in point of time, yet since a cause is prior to an effect in the order of nature, we usually speak of it as prior in point of time. Upon the same principle we speak of God's decrees in language borrowed from the relations which the objects of the decrees sustain to each other, though to His mind all things are "naked" and present. Hence, all the decrees of God are absolutely eternal, but the Scriptures speak of the eternity of election with marked and pointed emphasis: "According as He hath chosen us in Him before the foundation of the world," etc. Eph. i. 4. "According to His own purpose and grace which was given us in Christ Jesus before the world began." 2 Tim. i. 9. "Known unto God are all His works from the beginning of the world." Acts xv. 18.

5. The next point in the statement is the *sovereignty* of election, and here we enter upon that peculiar view of the doctrine which renders it so unpalatable to the carnal heart. There is, in all unrenewed minds, a scarcely acknowledged but secretly felt persuasion that God can be conciliated or brought under obligations to be propitious by their own legal performances. Men are unwilling to admit that their case is hope-

less without the intervention of sovereign mercy; they will not believe until persuaded to it by the Holy Spirit that they neither do nor can have any claims upon God, that they are just "vessels of wrath fitted for destruction," in themselves considered, and that the only ground of Divine favour is in the Divine Being Himself. But all our legal bias and propensities must be carefully dismissed while we attend with impartial ears to the testimony of Inspiration. What say the Scriptures? for whatever they say must be the truth. But before entering directly upon the Scripture testimony, it may be well to give a brief view of the sentiments of the Arminians, who, as Turrettin too justly remarks, "recall Popery and Pelagianism by the back door." They suspend the decree of personal election upon a foresight of faith and perseverance in holiness, and resolve both of these, in great measure, into a good use of the sinner's free will. "They make," says Turrettin, "the decree of election twofold: the first is general, being God's purpose to save all believers; the second is special, being His purpose to save such and such individuals who, He foresaw, would believe. The first they resolve entirely into the will of God; the second, though founded in the Divine will, attaches so much importance to faith as to make it the reason why one is elected and another not." The question between us and the Arminians respects simply the cause of election in the Divine mind—whether the decree is wholly unconditional, depending upon the mere good pleasure of God's will, or whether it is suspended upon a foresight of faith and perseverance in the creature. We do not deny that the decree of election includes the instrumentality of means in its accomplishment, and that faith and good works are indispensably necessary to its execution or fulfilment, but we do deny that faith, perseverance, good works, or any other thing in the creature, was the cause or reason why God elected one and passed by another; and we confidently appeal to the Scriptures of eternal truth to bear us out in our positions.

(1.) Faith is uniformly represented in the Bible as the

fruit or effect of election, and therefore cannot possibly be the cause of it. This point has already been fully established in the previous discussion of the nature of eternal life or salvation. It was there shown that a decree to save must mean a decree to bestow all the blessings of redemption, from the implantation of a new nature in regeneration to its full development in a state of glory. Having, then, already anticipated this point, I shall now dismiss it with only a few additional texts: "As many as were ordained to eternal life believed." Acts xiii. 48. It is the merest quibbling to interpret the *ordination* here of a disposition to believe, and it would probably puzzle those who do so to tell us whence the disposition arose. The word generally means "ordained or appointed," and accordingly these individuals are said to have believed because they were appointed to salvation. This is the natural and obvious meaning of the passage. "All that the Father giveth me shall come to me." John vi. 37. To come to Christ means to believe on Him, and faith is in this passage attributed by the Saviour Himself to election. Others did not believe because they were not of Christ's sheep; those who do believe must trace their faith to the sovereign goodness of God. The passage teaches us, moreover, that all who are given to Christ certainly shall believe, thus evidently throwing election farther back than faith. The truth then plainly is, that election is the cause of faith, and not faith of election.

(2.) This scheme, which suspends election upon foreseen faith and perseverance, amounts to a downright denial of the doctrine altogether, or, if there be any choice in the case at all, it is the sinner choosing God, and not God the sinner. Arminians represent faith and perseverance as prescribed conditions of salvation. The man, therefore, who complies with the conditions obtains the blessing promised upon a principle very different from that of election. It is an abuse of language to say that an individual under these circumstances is *chosen* to receive the blessing. The executive of the country issues a proclamation in which he offers a great reward to any individual who shall apprehend a notorious malefactor fleeing from justice. Some citizens do apprehend him and claim the reward. Is there any propriety in saying that they were elected to the reward? Nor would it affect the principle involved in the case at all to suppose that the executive knew beforehand precisely what individuals would apprehend the criminal. The Arminians, therefore, charge the Apostles and our Saviour Himself with an outrageous abuse and perversion of language when they represent them as using plain and familiar words in an acceptation which they cannot bear. There is much weight in the following remark of Turrettin: "If election depend upon foreseen faith, God cannot elect man, but man chooses God, and so predestination should rather be called postdestination—the first cause becomes the second, and God becomes dependent upon man, which is false and contrary to the nature of things, and Christ Himself testifies, 'ye have not chosen me, but I have chosen you.'" John xv. 16.

(3.) The Scriptures in so many words refer the cause of election to the sovereign pleasure of God, independently of any considerations derived from the creature. Eph. i. 5, 11: "Having predestinated us unto the adoption of children by Jesus Christ to Himself, *according to the good pleasure of His will;* in whom also we have obtained an inheritance, being predestinated according to the purpose of Him who worketh all things after *the counsel of His own will.*" 2 Tim. i. 9: "Who hath saved us and called us with an holy calling, not according to our works, but *according to His own purpose and grace,* which was given us in Christ Jesus before the world began." Titus iii. 5: "Not by works of righteousness which we have done, but according to His *mercy* He saved us," etc. These Scriptures require no comment; they are so plain and unambiguous that he who runs may read.

But the ninth chapter of the Epistle to the Romans is in a great measure a professed exposition of the absolute sovereignty of God in selecting the objects of His favour. Pelagians and Arminians have laboured diligently but unsuccessfully to neutralize the testimony of the Apostle in that chapter, and they have been somewhat encouraged by the partial concurrence of a few Calvinistic commentators in their views. They maintain that the Apostle is not speaking of a personal election to eternal life, but merely of a national election to external privileges—not of Jacob and Esau as individuals, but of their respective descendants as communities or nations. This interpretation rests principally upon the quotations from the Old Testament which Paul applies to the discussion, and upon a gratuitous assumption that Esau did not serve Jacob. The first passage of any great importance in the discussion is taken from Genesis xxv. 23: "Two nations are within thy womb, and the one people shall be stronger than the other people, and the elder shall serve the younger." Macknight, in his second note on Romans ix. 11, remarks: "The Apostle, according to his manner, cites only a few words of the passage on which his argument is founded, but I have inserted the whole in the commentary, to show that Jacob and Esau are not spoken of as individuals, but as representing the two nations springing from them—'Two nations are in thy womb,' etc.—and that the election of which the Apostle speaks is not an election of Jacob to eternal life, but of his posterity to be the visible Church and people of God on earth, and heirs of the promises in their first and literal meaning, agreeably to what Moses declared, Deut. vii. 6, 7, 8, and Paul preached, Acts. xiii. 17. That this is the election here spoken of appears from the following circumstances: 1. It is neither said, nor is it true of Jacob and Esau personally, that the elder served the younger. This is only true of their posterity. 2. Though Esau had served Jacob personally, and had been inferior to him in worldly greatness, it would have been no proof at all of Jacob's election to eternal life, nor of Esau's reprobation. As little was the subjection of the Edomites to the Israelites in David's days a proof of the election and reprobation of their progenitors. 3. The apostle's professed purpose in this discourse being to show that an election being bestowed on Jacob's posterity by God's free gift might either be taken from them, or others might be admitted to share therein with them, it is evidently not an election to eternal life, which is never taken away, but an election to external privileges only. 4. This being an election of the whole posterity of Jacob, and a reprobation of the whole descendants of Esau, it can only mean that the nation which was to spring from Esau should be subdued by the nation which was to spring from Jacob, and that it should not, like the nation springing from Jacob, be the Church and people of God, nor be entitled to the possession of Canaan, nor give birth to the Seed in whom all the families of the earth were to be blessed. 5. The circumstance of Esau's being older than Jacob was very properly taken notice of, to show that Jacob's election was contrary to the right of primogeniture, because this circumstance proved it to be from pure favour. But if his election had been to eternal life, the circumstance of his age ought not to have been mentioned, because it had no relation to that matter whatever." The next leading passage which Paul quotes is taken from Exodus xxxiii. 19 : " And He said I will make all my goodness pass before thee, and I will proclaim the name of the Lord before thee, and will be gracious to whom I will be gracious, and will show mercy to whom I will show mercy." " Here," says Macknight, " mercy is not an eternal pardon granted to individuals, but the receiving of a nation into favour after being displeased with it; for these words were spoken to Moses after God had laid aside His purpose of consuming the Israelites for their sin in making and worshipping the golden calf." "It is a notorious fact," says Bishop Sumner,[1] " though often overlooked in argument, that the very passage, ' I will have mercy on whom I will have mercy, and I will have compassion on whom I will have compassion,' which is almost

[1] Apostolic Preaching, p. 36.

the only support claimed from St. Paul to the system of absolute decrees, is quoted from Exodus, and forms the assurance revealed by God Himself to Moses that He had *separated the Hebrew nation* from all the people on the face of the earth." The next quotation is from Exodus ix. 16 : " And in very deed for this cause have I raised thee up, for to show in thee my power, and that my name may be declared throughout all the earth. In reference to this, Macknight observes: " Though Pharaoh alone was spoken to, it is evident that this and everything else spoken to him in the affair of the plague was designed for the Egyptian nation in general, as we learn from Exodus iv. 22 : ' Say unto Pharaoh, thus saith the Lord, Israel is my son, even my first-born.' 23 : ' And I say unto thee, let my son go that he may serve me, and if thou refusest to let him go, behold I will slay thy son, even thy first-born.' For, as Israel here signifies the nation of the Israelites, so Pharaoh signifies the nation of the Egyptians, and Pharaoh's son, even his first-born, is the first-born of Pharaoh and of the Egyptians. In like manner, Exodus ix. 15 : ' I will stretch out my hand that I may smite thee and thy people with pestilence, and thou shalt be cut off from the earth ;' that is, thou and thy people shall be cut off, for the pestilence was to fall on the people as well as on Pharaoh. Then follow the words quoted by the apostle, verse 16 : ' And in very deed,' etc. Now, as no person can suppose that the power of God was to be shown in the destruction of Pharaoh singly, but in the destruction of him and his people, this that was spoken to Pharaoh was spoken to him and to the nation of which he was the head."

I have thus given above, and mostly in the words of Macknight, the very marrow and pith of the Arminian argument. The notes which I have quoted contain the sum and substance of the more expanded observations of Sumner and Adam Clarke, who have laboured in the perversion of this celebrated chapter with a diligence and zeal worthy of a better cause. It will be seen at once that the principle upon which their reasoning proceeds is wholly gratuitous and false. They settle what they suppose to be the meaning of a passage in the Old Testament, and then determine that it cannot be used in any other sense in the New. Let the principle be tested by a reference to Matt. ii. 15, where Joseph is said to have departed into Egypt, "that it might be fulfilled which was spoken of the Lord by the prophet saying, Out of Egypt have I called my son." This last clause is clearly a quotation from Hosea xi. 1, where it has a manifest allusion to the children of Israel as a people or nation : "When Israel was a child then I loved him, and called my son out of Egypt." Upon the principle of interpretation on which Macknight proceeds the 15th verse of the second chapter of Matthew cannot refer to the Lord Jesus Christ, because the passage in Hosea will not bear that meaning; but every one sees from the context that it must and does refer to Christ, no matter what may be the meaning of the original passage in the Prophet. And so, if the scope and drift of the Epistle to the Romans show that Paul is discussing the question of a personal election to eternal life, no matter what may be the meaning of the original passages in Genesis and Exodus, the Apostle applies them to the subject before him. It is true that where an appeal is made to the Old Testament to *confirm* a truth delivered by an Evangelist or an Apostle, the words cannot be accommodated, but must be quoted in their original sense ; but it is equally true that the language of the Old Testament is often used by the writers of the New, just as we use the language of writers who have gone before us in the way of illustration and ornament. In such cases we may warrantably employ the language in a sense different from that in which it was originally used. It is certainly incumbent upon the Arminians therefore to show not only that the original passages quoted by Paul have reference to nations and not to individuals, but also to show that Paul has actually applied the passages in the identical sense of Moses. Their point is not gained by proving the first proposition without also proving the last. Besides all this, they must show that these passages are not referred to as containing undeniable proofs of a principle which was suited to the point in hand. So far from attempting to show this, Arminian commentators universally concede that God is sovereign in the distribution of national privileges; in other words, they admit the principle that God does distribute some blessings without respect to the character or works of individuals. May not Paul have been quoting the passages from the Old Testament merely because they teach this principle so peculiarly appropriate to the subject in hand? May not his reasoning have been something like this?—" We see that there is no injustice in God's bestowing peculiar blessings on some and rejecting others, because from His word that appears to be a principle of His government—a well-settled and established principle. He declares that He is not influenced by the merit of individuals, but by His own will. If this principle extend to the distribution of favours upon earth, there is no reason why it should not extend to the bestowment of eternal blessings. There are the same objections to the principle in the one case as in the other; and yet if God declares that He does act upon it in the one case, we infer from His unchangeableness that He must act upon it in the other. The difficulty lies, not against the character of the blessings bestowed, but against the sovereign nature of the choice." I can easily conceive that Paul might have applied the quotations from the Old Testament to the case of personal election, merely because they contain the *principle*, and the *whole principle*, upon which personal election depends. It is obvious, then, that even upon the supposition that the passages from Genesis and Exodus are correctly interpreted, it is not proved that Paul is not speaking in the ninth of Romans of personal election to eternal life. The point which Paul has in hand must be gathered, not from the writings of Moses, but from the scope and design of his own Epistle, and it only shows how hardly pressed the Arminians are when they overlook one of the simplest and most obvious rules of interpretation in order to avoid the truths which Paul so clearly teaches.

[1.] I am not prepared, however, to admit, though I believe Arminians would gain nothing by the admission, that the passages in the Old Testament refer exclusively to nations. On the contrary, I think that they manifestly teach a distinction between *individuals* as the ground of the distinction between nations. A careful examination of Genesis xxv. 23 will put this matter beyond all reasonable doubt. Rebecca, while pregnant, and probably somewhat advanced in pregnancy, seems to have felt a strange and unusual agitation in her womb, arising from the violent conflict of the twins, and, perplexed with a very natural anxiety, she consulted the Lord for instruction and relief. It is obvious that the contest of the brothers in the womb was altogether an extraordinary event, and was the certain presage of the future animosity which should distract and divide their descendants. The distinction between the nations, then, seems to have commenced in the womb. The answer of the Lord to Rebecca is decisive on this point: " Two nations are within thy womb;" that is, the children which are in thy womb shall become each the father of a nation. " And two manner of people shall be separated from thy bowels;" that is, two distinct and separate nations shall spring from the twins. Now, here the separation is said to take place from Rebecca's " bowels;" that is, from the children which were then in her womb. This teaches as plainly as language can teach that the distinction between the Edomites and Israelites supposed a previous distinction between Jacob and Esau as individuals. This again is confirmed by the unambiguous and pointed testimony of Malachi, who represents God's love to the Israelites as originating with God's love to Jacob as an individual. Besides, it is common in the Scriptures to trace the grace of God toward the Jews to His love for their fathers: " as touching the election, they are beloved for their fathers' sake." Rom. xi. 25. There is no violence, therefore, in applying this passage of Genesis to a distinction between Jacob and Esau as *individuals;* for it *does* teach such a distinction, and it is in this sense alone that Paul has quoted it: " For the *children* being not yet born," etc. v. 11. Here is nothing about *nations,* but *children.* But we are told that Esau never did serve Jacob, and therefore the passage cannot possibly apply to them as individuals. It may be answered that Jacob did obtain the birth-right, which was the blessing promised, and that Esau did upon several occasions acknowledge his inferiority to his brother. This was the spirit of the prophecy in regard to the individuals, though it had a fuller accomplishment in their respective descendants. But it is contended that if the prophecy did have a reference to the brothers as individuals, it would not follow that the distinction was that one was elected to eternal life, and the other reprobated and left to the sentence of eternal death. But if Paul is speaking of the brothers as individuals, it will follow that the ninth chapter of Romans has no reference to an election of nations to external privileges; it will overthrow the Arminian if it does not establish the Calvinistic interpretation. There are, however, good reasons for supposing that the birth-right was a type of spiritual blessings, as Canaan was a type of a heavenly country. Many of the events and personages of the Old Testament are certainly typical, and the Jewish people were constantly taught spiritual truths in the strong, impressive language of types. When we consider how little personal advantage Jacob gained in this world from obtaining the birth-right, it is natural to suppose that God's promise had reference to other and higher blessings. In fact, the election of the Jewish people themselves was a standing symbol of another and a nobler election. All the prominent transactions of God in reference to Canaan shadow forth the spiritual principles by which His Church is regulated and governed. The Exodus from Egypt, the Paschal Lamb, the journeyings in the wilderness, the crossing of Jordan, the settlement in Canaan and the expulsion of the Canaanites and surrounding tribes, are all typical of solemn and important spiritual events connected with the redemption of sinners by the Lord Jesus Christ. There is nothing unreasonable, therefore, in supposing that Jacob, under the type of the birth-right, *did* receive the gratuitous promise of eternal life, and that Esau was passed by and rejected. This certainly is the sense, as we shall presently see more fully, in which Paul quotes the passage, " the elder shall serve the younger." Macknight's third argument, in the first note quoted, is a mere begging of the question. He takes for granted what the Apostle's express design is, and then argues, from his own gratuitous assumption, against personal election to eternal life. The same is true of his fourth. In regard to the fifth, it may be remarked that the age of Jacob is mentioned to show how entirely free the election was—how completely independent of all considerations derived from the creature.

As to the passage in Exodus xxxiii. 19, it is wholly gratuitous to suppose that this was spoken in reference exclusively to the Jewish people. It is true that God spake these words after He had laid aside His purpose of consuming Israel for their idolatry, but this does not prove that the truth obtains only in particular circumstances. The immediate occasion of the words was the request of an individual. Moses said unto the Lord, " I beseech Thee, show me Thy glory." The 19th verse, which seems to be an answer to Moses' request, is a statement of the character of God considered in Himself : " I will make all my goodness pass before thee, and I will proclaim the name of the Lord before thee." This cannot mean God's goodness to *Israel*, but the goodness of the Divine character *generally*. It is not spoken to the nation, but to an individual, and that in answer to a particular request. The words are to be taken in their general sense, then, as expressive of Divine attributes. In fact, the whole verse is designed to state a proposition in regard to God which is always and universally true—that God is good and sovereign. God was showing Moses the " back parts" of His " glory," and it is all forced interpretation to confine the declarations to a particular form of the Divine goodness, as Macknight and Bishop Sumner have done. This is limiting what God has left absolute. There is no foundation for Sumner's remark, that this verse forms " the assurance revealed by God Himself to Moses that He had separated the Hebrew nation from all the people on the face of the earth;" for there is not a syllable about such a separation in the passage itself or in the immediate context.

The next quotation from Exodus (ix. 16) affords just as little ground for a national interpretation. It is manifest that the words themselves regard Pharaoh only as an individual: "And in very deed for this cause have I raised *thee* up for to show in *thee* my power," etc. It was Pharaoh's heart that was hardened, and the destruction of the Egyptians is represented as a punishment to Pharaoh himself. It was Pharaoh alone that could let Israel go, and Pharaoh is answerable for keeping them in bondage. Pharaoh is rejected from no national privileges; he is brought forward as a gross and flagitious sinner, stiffening his neck against God and setting at naught His authority. The whole transaction has not the remotest tendency to show that God elected Israel and passed by Egypt. God did not design to illustrate this principle in His dealings with Pharaoh, but to show His power and justice in casting down the proud and punishing the guilty; and for this purpose the case of this monarch is frequently alluded to in the sacred writings. True, Pharaoh was the head of his nation, and his guilt seriously affected his subjects; but how does this prove that God deals with him only as the representative of his people? The private sins of kings and emperors at the present day often involve their respective nations in sufferings and war, and yet their sins are personal and individual. Upon the whole, then, a correct view of the passages in the Old Testament does not bind us to believe that they have any necessary reference to the dealings of God with nations in respect to external privileges. Some necessarily apply to *individuals*, and all may be safely interpreted of them. The only possible foundation, therefore, on which a national interpretation of this chapter can rest is, to say the least, precarious and doubtful.

[2.] But should it be admitted that an election to the blessings or privileges of the external theocracy is all that is meant, the difficulty is by no means removed. " A choice," as Professor Hodge justly remarks, " to the blessings of the theocracy, that is, of a knowledge and worship of the true God, involved in a multitude of cases, at least, a choice to eternal life, as a choice to the means is a choice to the end. And it is only so far as these advantages were a means to this end that their value was worth considering." And again : " Is there any more objection to God's choosing men to a great than a small blessing on the ground of His own good pleasure ? The foundation of the objection is not the character of the blessings we are chosen to inherit, but the sovereign nature of the choice. Of course it is not met by making these blessings greater or less."

[3.] The whole scope of the Epistle goes to show that the Apostle is not speaking of a choice to external privileges. The first eight chapters are occupied in the doctrinal discussion of justification—the guilt and depravity which it supposes in our race, and the glorious blessings which are inseparably connected with it. These blessings are not mere outward privileges, but are *saving graces*—purity, holiness, peace with God and the certain hope of eternal life. These blessings are not bestowed on *nations*, but on *individuals*. It had, however, been a favourite prejudice of the Jewish nation that all the blessings of the Messiah's kingdom were to be exclusively confined to them, in virtue of God's covenant with Abraham. The Apostle, therefore, in the ninth chapter, begins the discussion of the question, Who are to be the subjects of Christ's kingdom ? Who are to be partakers of that " pardon, peace, and eternal life" which are found only in Jesus ? All the previous parts of the Epistle have been speaking of only one kind of privileges, and that the saving blessings of the Gospel. It is a violent presumption to suppose that Paul here drops all consideration of them, and begins a discussion about national advantages which have no conceivable connection with the scope and design of the Epistle. Unconnected as Paul is thought by many to be in his writings, such a transition would be altogether unpardonable. The question plainly before him was, Who shall be saved? Who shall be recipients of the hopes of the Gospel? This question is very naturally and obviously connected with the previous discussion. As in the solution of this question he was about to announce a very unwelcome truth to his brethren, he commences the chapter with cordial professions of attachment and love, manifested by the deep interest which he took in their spiritual welfare. He then delicately approaches the main point by anticipating an objection, verse 6: "Not as though the Word of God had taken none effect." That is, God was not bound by His promises to Abraham to bestow the blessings of the Gospel on the Jews, considered merely as natural descendants of the patriarch. Why? "They are not all Israel which are of Israel;" that is, the promises were made only to the spiritual seed, but all the natural descendants of Israel are not the spiritual seed. He then proves that natural descent did not entitle to the saving blessings of the Gospel, by a reference to the cases of Ishmael and Isaac, and of Esau and Jacob. The question then recurs, Who are the recipients of the promises? The answer is given in verse 8, which amounts to this: "Those who are born by a special interposition of God are the true individuals to whom the promises are effectual." But are these individuals confined to any particular nation, or found among any particular people? No. Ver. 24: They are those "whom He hath called, not of the Jews only, but also of the Gentiles." And here he begins the full disclosure of the solemn fact that many of his own countrymen, in spite of their privileges, would fail of eternal life, while many of the Gentiles would be admitted to the blessings of Messiah's kingdom. The observation of the Apostle in verse 24 is utterly inconsistent with the idea of a national election to external privileges, for he pointedly declares that the blessings of which he was then speaking are confined to no nation, but are extended to called or chosen ones in every nation: "Those whom He hath called, not of the Jews only, but also of the Gentiles"—those *persons* or *individuals* in every nation whom He hath chosen to eternal life. The Apostle here, as elsewhere, tells us that "there is no difference," no distinction in Christ's kingdom, of Jew and Greek —that "neither circumcision availeth anything, nor uncircumcision, but a new creature." To illustrate this great principle, that the recipients of the blessings of the Gospel are just those whom God chooses in His sovereign pleasure, is the design of the ninth chapter and the two following. In applying it to the Jews, he was obliged to reveal the rejection of many of his countrymen, and to establish, contrary to their prejudices, the calling and conversion of the Gentiles.

To any candid reader of this Epistle the evidence is cumulative that Paul does not refer to the choice of nations to peculiar privileges. In verse 3 he says: "For I could wish that myself were accursed from Christ for my brethren, my kinsmen according to the flesh." Now could the "heaviness" of Paul's heart on account of his brethren have been so great as to prompt such language as this, if his brethren after all were losing nothing but the privilege of being the exclusive people of God? Would Paul grieve so seriously and deeply because the Gentiles were admitted to equal privileges with the Jews? Can it be supposed for a moment that such language was or could have been penned by the inspired Apostle, when the whole grievance was that the middle wall of partition between Jew and Gentile was broken down, and that God was dispensing His Gospel to the ends of the earth? No! Paul saw a cloud filled with wrath—a black cloud of vindicatory justice affecting the eternal interests of his countrymen—ready to burst upon their heads; he saw many of them sealed up under the terrible judgment of judicial blindness, and in spite of their privileges going down to hell; and this it was which racked his heart with agony, and drew forth his thrilling expressions of sympathy and grief. He envied not the Gentiles; on the contrary, he makes their calling and conversion matters of solemn doxology and thanksgiving to God; but he did lament, deeply and sorely lament, that so many of his countrymen were cut off from the hopes of eternal life.

"The choice, moreover, is between vessels of mercy and vessels of wrath—vessels of mercy chosen unto '*glory*,' not unto church privileges, and vessels of wrath who were made the example of God's displeasure against sin."

In verses 30, 31, Paul states definitely the privileges which this election respected—justification by faith and its attendant blessings. "What shall we say then? That the Gentiles, which followed not after righteousness, have attained to righteousness, even the righteousness which is of faith. But Israel, which followed after the law of righteousness, hath not attained to the law of righteousness." It would certainly be a gross abuse of language to apply the phrases "righteousness which is of faith, law of righteousness," to mere external privileges; these phrases manifestly refer to the saving blessings of the Gospel, and yet it is this righteousness which a majority of the Jews forfeited, and which the Gentiles obtained by election.

The tenth chapter shows that the rejection of the Jews implied the loss of saving privileges. Paul commences it with a prayer that they "might be *saved*"—not that their national privileges might be retained, but that they might receive the gift of eternal life. He shows that they lose *justification*, not church privileges, by rejecting Christ and clinging to their own righteousness. Much of the chapter is taken up in discussing the plan of salvation and the nature and grounds of saving faith, but not a word concerns national privileges. The eleventh chapter bears a plain testimony to the fact that Paul was discussing matters of eternal life and eternal death. I shall just refer to the first verse. Here Paul denies that God has rejected the whole Jewish nation, and brings himself forward as an instance of a Jew who was not rejected. If the question respected only national privileges, an argument drawn from the case of an individual would be sheer nonsense. How could Paul possess *national* privileges? But Paul means to say that some of the Jews will be *saved*, or that all will not be lost, and in proof of this proposition he brings himself forward as an example of a converted Jew. That this is his meaning will appear from a comparison of verses 5 and 6, in which he asserts that there is a chosen remnant who will be saved, while the great majority of the nation was blinded. And in the conclusion of this protracted discussion, I would only observe that the interpretation for which I contend derives no small support from the objections which the Apostle considers against his own doctrines. They are those which in all ages have been urged against personal election to eternal life, but I do not know that they have ever been applied to the cases of nations or communities blessed above others with peculiar privileges.

These considerations are sufficient, it would seem, to satisfy any candid mind that in the ninth of Romans the Apostle is treating of a personal election to eternal life, and if so the texts are in point, and render it absolutely certain that election is wholly unconditional and sovereign. In fact, Arminians are aware of this, and therefore labour so strenuously to distort these Scriptures from their obvious application. In verse 11 it is said: "For the children being not yet born, neither having done any good or evil, that the purpose of God according to election might stand, not of works, but of Him that calleth, it was said unto her, The elder shall serve the younger." If language has any meaning at all, these verses teach that there is no other foundation of election than the mere mercy and goodness of God, which embrace whom He chooses of Adam's ruined race, without paying the least regard to works. Again, verse 15, it is said: "I will have mercy on whom I will have mercy, and I will have compassion on whom I will have compassion." "God," says Calvin, "proved by this very declaration that He is debtor to none; that every blessing bestowed upon the elect flows from gratuitous kindness, and is freely granted to whom He pleases; that no cause which is superior to His own will can be conceived or devised why He entertains kind feelings or manifests kind actions to some of the children of Adam and not to all." "So, then, it is not of him that willeth nor of him that runneth, but of God that showeth mercy." Verse 16. "These words," says Professor Hodge, "are not intended to teach that the efforts of men for the attainment of salvation are useless, much less do they teach that such efforts should not be made. They simply declare that the result is not to be attributed to them—that the reason why one man secures the blessing and another does not is not to be found in the greater ardour of desire or intensity of effort in the one than in the other, but the reason is in God."

The last passage which I shall quote to sustain the gratuitous election of God is found in Romans xi. 5–7: "Even so then at this present time also there is a remnant according to the election of grace. And if by grace then it is no more of works, otherwise grace is no more grace. But if it be of works, then it is no more grace; otherwise work is no more work. What then? Israel hath not obtained that which he seeketh for, but the election hath obtained it, and the rest were blinded." In order to avoid the force of this passage an interpretation has been devised utterly at war with all the principles of language. The gratuitous election here spoken of has been twisted to mean an election of *faith* as the condition of salvation rather than works. Out of all the possible plans which God might have adopted, He has selected that which makes faith in Christ the medium of justification, and this choice of faith is entirely gratuitous, faith having no more claims upon God's favour than works. "*Risum teneatis amici?*" It is sufficiently plain that the Apostle is not discussing the election of a principle, but of men; "the election"—that is, the elect or chosen ones—"have obtained it, and the rest were blinded." Can he mean that all the other possible schemes of salvation which God might have laid down instead of faith were blinded? And what strange jargon is it to talk of electing a principle! These pitiful subterfuges show how hard it is to close the eyes against a truth which Paul so plainly teaches—the solemn truth that God is free and sovereign in the distribution of His favours.

The separate points in the doctrine of election having been thus discussed, it may be well to make a few remarks on the inseparable doctrine of *reprobation*. The very fact that all men were not elected shows that some were passed by. This passing them by, or refusing to elect them, and leaving them under a righteous sentence of condemnation, constitutes reprobation. If election is personal, eternal and absolute, reprobation must possess these qualities also. There is this difference between them, however: election finds the objects of mercy unfit for eternal life, and puts forth a positive agency in preparing them for glory; reprobation finds the objects of wrath already fitted for destruction, and only withholds that influence which alone can transform them. It is not intended to deny here that cases of judicial blindness occur in which the sinner's heart is hardened. The example of Pharaoh is a case in point. But judicial blindness is a *punishment* inflicted in which God acts as a righteous Judge dealing with men for their obstinacy; whereas reprobation is strictly an act of sovereignty in which God refuses to save, and leaves the sinner to the free course of law. Our Standards afford no sort of shelter to the Hopkinsian error that the decree of reprobation consists in God's determining to fit a certain number of mankind for eternal damnation, and that the Divine agency is as positively employed in men's bad volitions and actions as in their good. These doctrines, we know, have been frequently charged upon us with no little violence and acrimony, but we have always adhered to the position of the Bible, that God is not the author of evil; and we believe that there is no inconsistency in supposing that

God may determine an action as a natural event, and yet be unstained with its sin and pollution. That the Scriptures teach the doctrine of reprobation, as depending on the sovereignty and good pleasure of God, is manifest from the following passages—Matt. xi. 25: "At that time Jesus answered and said, I thank thee, O Father, Lord of heaven and earth, because Thou hast hid these things from the wise and prudent, and hast revealed them unto babes." Here our blessed Saviour addresses the Father by a word highly expressive of sovereignty, and refers the illumination of some and the blindness of others to His Father's will alone: "Even so, Father, for so it seemed good in Thy sight." Rom. ix. 18: "Therefore hath He mercy on whom He will have mercy, and whom He will He hardeneth." If it be said that this refers to the judicial blindness with which Pharaoh was struck, let it be remembered that no punishment of any sort would or could be inflicted on the wicked, if they were not left under the sentence of condemnation originally pronounced upon the race. The fact of their reprobation leaves them in that state to which punishment was justly due, and the argument of Paul is that some are left in that state and others not by the sovereign pleasure of God. Verse 21: "Hath not the potter power over the clay, of the same lump to make one vessel unto honour and another to dishonour?" Jude 4: "For there are certain men crept in unawares, who were before of old ordained to this condemnation—ungodly men, turning the grace of our God into lasciviousness, and denying the only Lord God and our Lord Jesus Christ." In fact, every passage of Scripture which teaches that any will be finally lost, teaches at the same time, by necessary implication, if the doctrine of election be true, that they were eternally reprobated or left out of the number of the elect. The two doctrines stand or fall together.

Independently of the direct and immediate testimony which the Scriptures bear in support of eternal and unconditional election and reprobation, there is an indirect teaching of them by the inculcation of doctrines in which they are necessarily involved—such as the foreknowledge, providence and independence of God, and the total depravity of man. There is no way in which these truths can be reconciled with the Arminian or Semi-Pelagian scheme. Foreknowledge of a future event means, if it mean anything, that the event is regarded as absolutely certain in the Divine mind, and that it cannot possibly happen otherwise than as God foresees it will happen. How the absolute certainty of events is consistent with contingency, which necessarily implies uncertainty, I leave it to the advocates of that strange hypothesis to determine. The Scripture account of foreknowledge is simple and consistent: God foreknows all things because He decrees them, and hence the terms are frequently interchanged. Peter says that Christ was delivered to death "by the determinate counsel and foreknowledge of God;" that is, by the purpose and appointment of God. The doctrine of providence, by which God is represented as acting upon a plan of which He knew the end from the beginning, cannot be conceived at all if we deny the existence of a fixed and definite purpose in the Divine mind. In fact, the denial of an eternal purpose is a virtual dethronement of God in His own dominions; and the voice of reason remonstrates, as loudly as the voice of revelation, against the ruinous results to which such a denial must lead. The will of God becomes fearfully dependent upon the will of man, and the counsel of God must be formed and modelled upon the wisdom of the creature. The truth is, Arminianism declares an open war upon the essential attributes of God, and, if carried out into all its necessary consequences, it would lead at once to blank and cheerless Atheism.

The account which the Bible gives us of human corruption and depravity is utterly inconsistent with the scheme which makes election, in any measure, dependent upon the faith or perseverance of man. Sinners, in their natural state, are said to be "dead in trespasses and sins." "Every imagination of man's heart is only evil, and that continually." The necessary consequence of depravity is an utter inability to think a good thought or to perform a good action. The understanding is darkened, the affections alienated, the will bent on evil; in short, the man is dead, spiritually dead, and therefore cannot believe or do any holy action until quickened and renewed by the supernatural grace of God. Hence our Saviour says, "No man can come to Me, except the Father which hath sent Me draw him." If this, then, be the true state of the case, all who believe are drawn by the Father, being utterly unable to do it of themselves. Why does God draw one and not another?—for it is manifest that all are not believers. Every Christian will promptly ascribe his calling and conversion to the mere grace of God, and this is election. The man who rejects election is bound to reject the scriptural account of human depravity if he would maintain consistency of opinion. He may resort to the superficial theory of common grace, but that will not relieve him of his difficulty. The Scriptures attribute *every* good disposition to God, and so the disposition not to resist common grace must after all be referred to special grace. No Christian would ever have dreamed of Arminianism if he had been guided only by his own experience; hence, when the love of system is laid aside, we find all pious Arminians sober and honest-hearted Calvinists, as their earnest prayers for grace and assistance unequivocally declare.

Another source of argument on this subject is the whole course of Divine Providence, which shows that God is absolutely sovereign in the distribution of His favours. The Lord does not deal with all men alike. The election of the Jews to church privileges, and to their relation to God as His peculiar people, was founded solely on His gratuitous mercy. Moses again and again admonishes them that their exaltation was due to God's unmerited love, and the more effectually to check their pride and humble their hearts, "he reproaches them with having deserved no favour, but as being a stiff-necked and rebellious people." At this day millions of our fellow-men, no worse by nature than we, and no more unworthy of Divine compassion, are sunk in idolatry, degradation and ruin, while we enjoy the light of the Gospel and the privileges of the sanctuary. Why is this? It can only be resolved into the sovereign pleasure of God. Even amongst us some are born to affluence, honour and distinction, while others by the sweat of their brow can hardly procure a scanty subsistence for themselves and their families. Some are endowed with extraordinary powers of intellect, while others exhibit the melancholy spectacle of drivelling idiotcy. Why these distinctions among men whose moral characters are naturally the same? No other answer can be given but the sovereign pleasure of God. The Divine sovereignty in the distribution of favours is written in broad and palpable characters upon all His dealings with men and nations in the present course of His providence, and shall it be thought a thing incredible that the same principle should extend to their eternal interests? Has God the right to bestow or withhold temporal blessings, and not the right to bestow eternal blessings? The very same objections which may be raised against an election to life lie with all their force against the inequalities of Providence. The very same arguments which are adduced to prove that one man cannot be chosen to spiritual privileges while another is rejected, apply just as strongly to the point that one man cannot be born rich and another poor. The objections are raised to the nature of the choice, and not to the character of the blessings bestowed or withheld.

There is no other scheme which can be reconciled with the doctrine of salvation by free grace. If anything be left for the sinner to do, no matter how slight or insignificant the work may be, the blessing ceases to be the *gift* of God and becomes a matter of pactional debt. The Apostle testifies, however, that eternal life is the gift of God through the righteousness of Christ. Arminians endeavour to avoid the difficulty by maintaining that the intrinsic value of salvation far exceeds the merit of our works, so that the latter cannot be regarded as deserving the former; and inasmuch as our faith and repentance are not a strict equivalent for the blessings of life, in a comparative sense our works are not meritorious. But suppose a man should expose for sale an article worth a thousand dollars at the small price of one cent; the man who pays the one cent becomes entitled to the article on the score of debt just as completely as though he had paid the full value. The principle of debt is just this: a reward in consideration of something done. It matters not how slight that something may be. Now, when salvation is said to be by grace in opposition to works or debt, it excludes everything in the sinner himself as the ground of his title to it, and leaves it to the mere disposal of God, so that it shall not be of him that willeth nor of him that runneth, but of God that showeth mercy; and this is the very principle upon which election turns.

III. When the doctrines of absolute and unconditional election and reprobation are proclaimed, the perverse and rebellious hearts of the children of men are ready to conjure up a thousand objections against them. There is seldom any attempt made to overthrow the mass of positive, direct testimony in their favour, drawn alike from the Scriptures of truth, the character of God, the experience of the Christian and the uniform course of Divine Providence, because this is felt to be absolutely impossible. A less ingenuous method is resorted to. The prejudices of the carnal heart against the truth are diligently fostered; horrible consequences, revolting alike to reason and common sense, are perversely deduced; hobgoblin terrors are excited; bold and reckless assertion is substituted for argument; and all this miserable artifice is passed off as a refutation of Calvinism. Take away from many Arminian writers their gross misrepresentations and disgraceful personal abuse, their pompous rhodomontade against the "horrible decree," and their fiery declamation against consequences which exist nowhere but in their own brains, and what is left will be but a small portion compared with the whole. It seems to be forgotten that mere *objections*, which constitute at best but a negative testimony, cannot destroy positive evidence. If the truth is to be sacrificed to difficulties, what will become of the doctrines of the Trinity, of the incarnation of the Son, and of the residence of the Spirit in the hearts of believers? A thousand objections have been raised against these glorious truths just as plausible and fully as forcible as the objections of the Arminians against the doctrine of election; and yet no Christian would think of doubting them, because, though encumbered with difficulties, they are sustained by adequate testimony and confirmed by positive evidence.

The great source of error in regard to Divine things is ignorance. We are ignorant of God as He is in Himself, and ignorant of the full economy of His government. "Ye do err, not knowing the Scriptures nor the power of God," was the reply of our Saviour to the captious Sadducees when they brought forward what they conceived to be an unanswerable argument against the resurrection of the dead. The same reply may be justly given to those who are rebellious against the sovereignty of God, and it ought to be sufficient. If the Scriptures teach the doctrine, we may rest satisfied that all our difficulties arise from our ignorance; not from the subject itself in its own intrinsic nature, but from our limited faculties and still more limited knowledge. With this general observation the whole subject might be dismissed; but as a mode so summary of treating objections might have a tendency to magnify them in the minds of some beyond their just importance, it will probably be well to give the more prominent and common ones a fuller discussion. Let it not be supposed, however, that objections lie exclusively against the Calvinistic system. Men make but a poor exchange in the way of difficulties when they renounce the good old doctrines of the Reformation for the superficial schemes which depend essentially upon the sinner's free will. Arminians talk as confidently of the difficulties of Calvinism as if their own system were perfectly disencumbered of all objection, when the truth is that it has many difficulties in common with Calvinism, besides others peculiar to itself.

The leading objections to the doctrine of election are drawn from the moral character of God and from the moral agency of man. We shall consider them in order.

First. The attributes of God which are supposed to be injured by this doctrine are, His *justice,* His *impartiality,* and His *truth.* It is enough to make the blood run cold to read the terms of shocking and revolting blasphemy in which these objections are sometimes brought forward; and, I must believe, in many instances only for effect.

1. It is a standing theme of Arminian declamation that election and reprobation are utterly inconsistent with the justice of God; in other words, that God cannot be sovereign in fixing the destinies of men without ceasing to be just. It seems to be forgotten that there are two recorded notices in Scripture of this very objection: (1.) "What shall we say then? Is there unrighteousness with God? God forbid." Rom. ix. 14. Paul had, as we have already seen, been asserting in unlimited terms the very doctrine for which we are contending, and here, in verse 14, notices an objection which he was sure the flesh would bring up: "Is there unrighteousness with God?" "How prodigious," says Calvin, "is the frenzy of the human mind, which rather accuses God of injustice than convicts itself of being influenced by blindness!" It is observable that Paul, in answering this objection, simply appeals to the Scriptures of eternal truth. He shows that God, in so many words, claimed to be sovereign in the distribution of His favours, and appeals to a celebrated instance in which that sovereignty, in the withholding of favours, was actually exercised. He takes it for granted that the Scriptures are true, and that whatever God does must necessarily be right. No matter in what difficulties or obscurity the Divine dispensations may seem to be involved, yet God is essentially *just*, and therefore cannot do an unrighteous act. Now, the Scriptures *do* declare that God " hath mercy

on whom He will have mercy, and whom He will He hardeneth;" therefore such a procedure cannot possibly be *unjust*. God does it, *and on that account* it must be right. This is the sum and substance of Paul's answer to the objection, and it ought to be satisfactory to every pious mind. "The thought," as Calvin well observes in explaining the answer of Paul, "deserves the utmost execration which believes injustice to exist in the Fountain of all righteousness." And again: "The apology produced by Paul to show that God was not unjust, because He is merciful to whom He thinks fit, might appear cold; but because God's own authority, as it requires the aid and support of no other, is abundantly sufficient of itself, Paul was content to leave the Judge of quick and dead to avenge His own right." I cannot forbear to notice here how conclusively this objection evinces that Paul's doctrine and ours are precisely the same. "It clearly proves that the cause of God's rejecting some and electing others is to be sought for merely in His will and purpose; for if the difference between these two characters depended upon a regard to their works, Paul would have discussed the question concerning God's injustice in a very unnecessary manner, since no suspicion could possibly arise against the perfect justice of the Disposer of all things if He treats every son and daughter of Adam according to their works." If the Scriptures do really teach this doctrine, it cannot injure the justice of God, for the same Scriptures as clearly teach that God is *just*. If we have any regard for the authority of inspiration, we are bound to believe *both* truths. Suppose we cannot reconcile them or understand how they are reconciled, what then? It only follows that we are blind and short-sighted, and "cannot see afar off." The objection, then, according to the showing of an inspired Apostle, is good for nothing. But (2.) we have another authority on this subject. The Son of God Himself has condescended to notice this objection, and, in effect, to pronounce it utterly worthless. He put forth a parable, recorded in the twentieth chapter of Matthew, for the purpose of showing that God might distribute peculiar and special favours to some, without being guilty of any sort of injustice to others.

The scope of this whole parable is definitely stated in the sixteenth verse: "So the last shall be first, and the first last; for many be called, but few chosen." The terms *first* and *last*, in a spiritual sense, are applied to those who, in the judgment of men, would naturally be expected to be first or last in receiving the blessings of the Gospel. The "*first*" are those who, in consequence of peculiar endowments or adventitious circumstances, would seem to have the fairest claims upon the Divine clemency. They are sober, intelligent, respectable moral men. The "*last*" are those who notoriously have no shadow of claim, even in the carnal judgment of men, upon the compassion of God. They are decidedly and openly wicked. The moral and scrupulous but yet self-righteous Jews may be taken as a fair specimen of those whom our Saviour meant by the "first;" the abandoned publicans and harlots may be regarded as appropriate examples of those whom He intended by the "last." We should have expected *a priori* that the rigid descendants of Abraham would give a more ready and welcome reception to the Gospel than the profligate publicans or abandoned harlots; but yet facts, and the positive assertion of the Saviour, show that the last were first, and the first last. The same general truth is taught by Paul, 1 Cor. i. 26, 27: "For ye see your calling, brethren, how that not many wise men after the flesh, not many mighty, not many noble are called; but God has chosen the foolish things of the world to confound the wise, and God has chosen the weak things of the world to confound the things which are mighty," etc. Here Paul's wise men after the flesh, his noble and mighty, are the same with our Saviour's first, while his foolish and weak are the same with our Saviour's last. What is the reason that the first are last and the last first? "Many are called, but few chosen." "God hath *chosen*," etc., says Paul. The meaning, then, of verse 16, which contains the scope of the whole parable, is simply this : While all are freely invited to partake of the blessings of the Gospel, yet the sovereign choice of God applies them effectually, not to those who, according to the carnal judgment of men, would seem to have the greatest claim on the Divine mercy, but to those whose utter destitution of all shadow of claim would render God's grace the more remarkably conspicuous. To illustrate this principle, which has been frequently exemplified in the history of the Church, and to show that it is by no means inconsistent with the Divine justice, seems to be the special purpose of the parable. Our Saviour begins : " For the kingdom of heaven is like unto a man that is an householder, which went out early in the morning to hire labourers into his vineyard." Ver. 1. That is, the principle on which the saving blessings of the Gospel are conferred on men may be illustrated by the case of a householder in employing and rewarding labourers in his vineyard. " And when he had agreed with the labourers for a penny a day, he sent them into his vineyard. And he went out about the third hour, and saw others standing idle in the market-place, and said unto them, Go ye also into the vineyard, and whatsoever is right I will give you ; and they went their way. Again he went out about the sixth and ninth hour and did likewise. And about the eleventh hour he went out and found others standing idle, and saith unto them, Why stand ye here all the day idle ? They say unto him, Because no man hath hired us. He saith unto them, Go ye also into the vineyard, and whatsoever is right that shall ye receive." Verses 2–7. The circumstances of standing in the market-place and hiring labourers are merely ornamental, being designed to give life and costume to the narrative, but they have no immediate connection with its scope. It is idle, therefore, to attempt to seek, in our spiritual relations to God, anything to correspond with these minute particulars. The general truth designed to be conveyed is that the Lord is our common Master, and that we have no claims whatever upon Him except those to which He gives rise by His own gratuitous promise. The labourers had no claim to the patronage and bounty of the householder, and after he had employed them they had no right to expect a liberality from him beyond the terms of their engagement. Their relations to him required on his part nothing more than *sheer justice*. This was all they could ask. It may be asked here, What is meant by labouring in the vineyard? I answer that our Saviour by this meant simply to designate the relations in which men stand to God. These are two-fold—legal or gracious, according to the covenant under which men are. As the labourers in the vineyard were dealt with on the principles of justice or mercy, according to the light or relationship in which the householder chose to regard them, so men are dealt with by God upon the same principles, according to the relations in which they stand to Him. The labouring in the vineyard is a circumstance in the narrative designed to teach only a relationship, without specifying precisely what it is, or at all intimating that it was the same in all. This is most obvious from the sequel of the narrative. Suffice it to say, that we all stand to God in the general relationship of subjects to a sovereign, without having any right or title to clemency and grace. " So when the even was come, the Lord of the vineyard said unto his steward, Call the labourers and give them their hire, beginning from the last unto the first. And when they came that were hired about the eleventh hour, they received every man a penny. But when the first came they supposed that they should have received more, but they likewise received every man a penny." Verses 8–10. Here the point of resemblance between the kingdom of heaven and the householder is introduced, and here the *principle* on which the destinies of men are determined is clearly developed. That principle is simply this : God does injustice to none, while He is peculiarly merciful to some. The householder gave the labourers first employed their *due*. He was just to them, he withheld nothing to which they had any claim. So God will eventually give reprobate sinners their *due;* "the wages of sin is death;" they virtually agreed for this, for they knew the necessary consequence of guilt, and therefore God does them no injustice. On the other hand, the labourers last employed, who represent the elect, are treated far beyond their deserts ; they are dealt with on a principle of mercy, and through grace receive what they have no personal right to expect. It will be observed here that the labourers first employed answer, in the spiritual sense of the narrative, to those who seem to have some claims to the clemency and grace of God, while the labourers last employed answer to those who are notoriously destitute of all shadow of claim. It will be further observed that the penny simply denotes the idea of *wages,* for that was the customary hire of a day-labourer. From the fact that all received a penny we are simply to understand that all were fairly and honourably reckoned with. Some were dealt with on the principle of justice, receiving the stipulated wages of day-labourers ; others on the principle of mercy, receiving what they had no right to expect. In a spiritual sense the penny in one case would be death, the stipulated wages of sin ; in the other, eternal life, the stipulated reward of grace. "And when they had received it, they murmured against the good man of the house, saying, These last have wrought but one hour, and thou hast made them equal unto us, which have borne the burden and heat of the day." Verses 11, 12. The force of this objection is this : We have greater claims upon your kindness than the others ; we have been moral, upright men, and in many cases had a zeal for God, while these others have in too many instances been mere publicans and harlots, the ignorant and abandoned of society. Our claim is as much greater than theirs as the claim of labourers who have "borne the burden and heat of the day" is greater than the claim of idlers who have laboured only one hour. They no more compare with us in the qualifications suited to recommend them to God than such an idler can compare with such a labourer.

The men, it will be observed, who had laboured longest in the vineyard were literally first, and so had, it would seem, the fairest claim on the favour of the householder, but he judged differently, and consequently made the last first: "But he answered one of them and said, Friend, I do thee no wrong. Didst thou not agree with me for a penny? Take that thine is and go thy way. I will give unto this last even as unto thee. Is it not lawful for me to do what I will with mine own? Is thine eye evil because I am good? So the last shall be first, and the first last; for many be called, but few chosen." Verses 13–16. Here the proposition is flatly maintained that goodness to one implies no injustice to another in the case supposed. The reasons are—(1.) Because God is absolutely sovereign, and can do as He pleases in perfect consistency with justice. (2.) Because sinners have no claims upon God whatever. (3.) Because they are actually dealt with according to the demands of justice—just as much so as if they had stipulated with God for the punishment which they will ultimately receive.

To say nothing of the first, the two last points of our Saviour's answer contain a triumphant refutation of this vaunting objection, and therefore we shall consider them a little more particularly. The *first* position is that sinners have no sort of claim upon the Divine clemency. It has been already shown sufficiently that men in the decree of election and reprobation were regarded as fallen in Adam. The fall, being a breach of the covenant of law, brought the whole race under the sentence of condemnation and death. "By the offence of one judgment came upon all men to condemnation." Rom. v. 18. "And were by nature the children of wrath even as others." Eph. ii. 3. The only question of any importance here is, Was this a *righteous* sentence? The fact that God pronounced it is a sufficient answer. Now if the whole race were righteously condemned in the first instance, there could be no injustice in leaving them under the sentence and in actually inflicting the curse.

If the sentence itself was right, the execution of it cannot be wrong. God might, then, most justly and righteously have left every son and daughter of Adam to the terrible course of law, and if He could have left all indiscriminately, surely He can leave some, and yet be just and righteous still. But the sinner is not only legally and righteously condemned, but he is also desperately corrupt. His heart is deceitful above all things, being wholly alienated from God, and holiness, and heaven. He is absolutely *fit* by native depravity for nothing but banishment and eternal separation from his Maker. His mind is *enmity* against God, and therefore if introduced into heaven without a moral renovation he would be supremely miserable. His deep and malignant depravity is an object of abhorrence to God and to all holy beings, and the fact that he has destroyed himself cuts him off from all claim to the sympathy and compassion of the Being whom he has so grievously offended. The following remarks of Calvin deserve a serious and attentive consideration, and they are purposely introduced because that great and good man has been egregiously calumniated on this point: "Therefore, if any one attack us with such an inquiry as this, Why God has from the beginning predestinated some men to death who, not yet being brought into existence, could not yet deserve the sentence of death, we will reply by asking them in return, What they suppose God owes to man if He chooses to judge of him from his own nature? As we are all corrupted by sin, we must necessarily be odious to God, and that not from tyrannical cruelty, but in the most equitable estimation of justice. If all whom the Lord predestinates to death are in their natural condition liable to the sentence of death, what injustice do they complain of receiving from him? Let all the sons of Adam come forward; let them all contend and dispute with their Creator because by His eternal providence they were previously to their birth adjudged to endless misery. What murmur will they be able to raise against this vindication when God, on the other hand, shall call them to a review of themselves? If they have all been taken from a corrupt mass, it is no wonder that they are subject to condemnation. Let them not, therefore, accuse God of injustice if His eternal decree has destined them to death, to which they feel themselves, whatever be their desire or aversion, spontaneously led forward by their own nature. Hence appears the perverseness of their disposition to murmur, because they intentionally suppress the cause of condemnation which they are constrained to acknowledge in themselves, hoping to excuse themselves by charging it upon God." These two facts—that sinners are by nature odious and loathsome to God, and are under a righteous sentence of condemnation and death—establish beyond all doubt the position of the Saviour that none have any claims upon the Divine clemency or mercy. The *second* position is, that reprobate sinners are actually dealt with according to the demands of justice. God withholds nothing from them to which they have any claim, and He inflicts a punishment no more severe than they had every reason to expect. They are doomed to hell, but is not that the righteous allotment of the wicked? They are banished everlastingly from the presence of God, but did they not despise His authority, and were they not alienated in heart and affection from Him? Where is or can be the injustice of punishing the wicked? It is true that God withholds from them saving grace, because they have no right to expect it and He is under no obligation to bestow it. There is no *injustice* here—no more than there is *injustice* in my withholding alms from a beggar who despises me and calumniates my family.

Such seem to be the sentiments contained in the reply of our adorable Redeemer. But it may be said that justice is violated in the case of the elect, because they do not receive the punishment which is due to them. The answer is obvious: their glorious Substitute and Surety became a curse for them in order to redeem them from the curse of the law. Jesus suffered in their name and stead, and completely satisfied the demands of justice, so that God can be just and yet the justifier of all who believe on His Son. In neither case, then, is the justice of God violated. Upon the reprobate it has free course, and they endure in their own proper persons the tremendous penalty of the law. Upon the elect it has free course in the person of their adorable Head, and He endured the unutterable curse of the law. May we not, therefore, triumphantly ask with Paul, "Is there unrighteousness with God? God forbid."

I know that there are caricatures of Calvinism which represent God as having made man for the specific purpose of damnation, and as putting forth a positive agency in fitting him for hell. The reprobate are represented as poor, helpless, dependent creatures in the hands of a bloodthirsty tyrant, who, in the first instance, makes them sinners contrary to their own will, absolutely forcing them into transgression, and then, in spite of all their efforts, drives them to hell, that he may delight himself with their torments; and in such caricatures the reprobate are often represented as most *amiable* and *lovely* creatures, suited by their excellencies to soften a heart of stone; but yet the cruel God of the Calvinists frowns upon them and sends them down to hell. These gross and slanderous caricatures might pass unnoticed if they were not palmed off upon the ignorant and unthinking as the genuine doctrines of Presbyterianism. And the worst part of the whole is, that when Presbyterians disavow them, instead of being believed or regarded as fair judges of their own principles, they are only charged with disgraceful cowardice, or taunted with being ashamed of their doctrines. If it is to such caricatures that the charge of injustice is so confidently brought up, I have no motive to attempt an answer. It is enough that the charge cannot be sustained against the genuine doctrines of the Church.

2. Another very common but groundless objection to Calvinism is, that it imputes partiality to God, or makes Him a respecter of persons, while the Scriptures, on the other hand,

declare that God is " no respecter of persons." Now, there is no inconsistency at all in God's appointing some to life and others to death of His own sovereign will, and at the same time being " no respecter of persons," in the scriptural sense of the phrase. " By the word *person* the Scripture signifies not a man, but those things in a man which, being conspicuous to the eyes, usually conciliate favour, honour and dignity, or attract hatred, contempt and disgrace. Such are riches, wealth, power, nobility, magistracy, country, elegance of form, on the one hand ; and on the other hand, poverty, necessity, ignoble birth, slovenliness, contempt and the like. Thus Peter and Paul declare that God is not a respecter of persons, because He makes no difference between the Jew and the Greek, to reject one and receive the other merely on account of his nation. So James uses the same language when he means to assert that God in His judgment pays no regard to riches. And Paul, in another place, declares that, in judging, God has no respect to liberty or bondage." According to this definition or explanation of the phrase, God cannot be regarded as a respecter of persons, unless His choice of some and rejection of others turn upon something in the individuals themselves. But we have already seen that God in this matter is wholly uninfluenced by anything in man—He acts according to His *own will.* The motives to favour are derived solely from *His mere mercy.* If the motives of Divine action are derived entirely from the Divine Being Himself, He has manifestly no respect to persons, but only to His own will. The Scriptures declare that God loved Jacob and hated Esau, but they declare at the same time that there was nothing in Jacob to conciliate Divine favour more than in his brother. Now, if God were determined in bestowing His favours by the birth, or blood, or rank, or respectability, or station of men, He would be a respecter of persons ; but we have already seen that not many wise or noble or honourable are called. So far is His favour from being regulated by respect to persons. But it may be asked, Why does He not treat all alike ? I would answer this question by asking a few others. Has not God an unquestionable right to manifest His mercy? or is mercy wholly denied to Him? Has He not an equal right to exercise His justice? or is that attribute also denied to Him? If He has a right to exercise both attributes, may He not do it upon any subjects that in their own nature are fit to display them? If man is guilty, may not God exercise His justice in punishing? if miserable, may not God exercise His mercy in saving? If man is a fit subject for the display of both attributes, may not God choose some men for the manifestation of His mercy, and others for the manifestation of His justice? An affirmative answer cannot be withheld without denying one of the following propositions: Man is not a fit subject either of wrath or mercy; or, God cannot manifest His justice and grace. Men must take one horn of this dilemma, or confess that the Lord's ways are equal, even though He has mercy on whom He will have mercy, and whom He will He hardeneth. Calvin, with his usual ability, observes: "The Lord, therefore, may give grace to whom He will, because He is merciful; and yet not give it to all, because He is a just Judge; may manifest His free grace by giving to some what they never deserve, while by not giving to all He declares the demerit of all."

3. The doctrine of election is supposed to be inconsistent with the sincerity of God in the general invitations and call of the Gospel, and with His professions of willingness that all should be saved. It is true that this doctrine is wholly irreconcilable with the idea of a fixed determination on the part of God to save, indiscriminately, the whole human race. The plain doctrine of the Presbyterian Church is that God has no purpose of salvation for all, and that He has not decreed that faith, repentance and holiness, and the eternal blessings of the Gospel, should be efficaciously applied to all. The necessary consequence of such a decree would be universal salvation. The Scriptures, which are supposed to prove that God sent His Son into the world with the specific intention of saving all without exception or limitation, it is

confidently believed, teach, when correctly interpreted, no such doctrine. It is often forgotten that *love* is ascribed to God under two or three different aspects. Sometimes it expresses the complacency and approbation with which He views the graces which His own Spirit has produced in the hearts of His children; and in this sense it is plain that God can be said to love only the saints. It is probably in this sense that the term *love* is to be understood in Jude's exhortation: "Keep yourselves in the love of God." Sometimes God's *benevolence* or general mercy is intended, such as He bestows upon the just and the unjust, the evil and the good, as in Psalms cxlv. 9: "The Lord is good to all, and His tender mercies are over all His works." The common bounties of Providence may be referred to this head. Sometimes it expresses that peculiar and distinguishing favour with which He regarded His elect from all eternity. In this sense, the love of God is always connected with the purpose of salvation. Again, the word sometimes denotes nothing more than God's willingness to be reconciled to sinners in and through Christ. In regard to the love of complacency or approbation, it is manifest at once that unconverted sinners have no lot nor part in it. God is angry with them every day; "He hateth all workers of iniquity." The special love of God is confined exclusively to the elect. The general benevolence of God is common, but it implies no purpose of salvation at all; and therefore, in that sense, God may be said to love the reprobate and disobedient. Even the vessels of wrath fitted to destruction are borne with in much long-suffering and patience. In reference to the last, it is plain that God may be heartily willing to save sinners in and through Christ—may determine to save all, in other words, who receive the Saviour—without positively decreeing to create in all men the necessary faith. In this sense, therefore, God may be said to love sinners, for whom, however, He has no purpose of salvation. Having established an inseparable connection between faith and salvation, He will infallibly save all that believe; but it by no means follows that He will certainly bestow faith on all to whom the Gospel is preached. Hence, another important distinction, to be borne in mind, is between what is technically called by divines the εὐαρεστία of God and His εὐδοκία. By the first is meant that which God commands and is agreeable to His precept—in other words, what He requires His creatures to do; by the other is meant His own fixed purpose or decree, or what He actually intends to do Himself. The distinction is sometimes expressed by the terms *preceptive* and *decretive*, applied to the will of God. It was the preceptive will of God that the Jews should not crucify the Lord Jesus Christ. They acted in this matter contrary to God's command, and were therefore guilty; still, it was His decretive will that the Saviour should be crucified, for the Jews and Roman soldiers did only what "His hand and His counsel determined before to be done." The preceptive will of God is the rule of duty to us; the decretive will, the plan of operations to Himself. The distinction is plainly just, natural and scriptural.

The preceptive will of God is sometimes called His *revealed* will, and His decretive called His *secret* will. This distinction does not suppose that the will of God in itself is compound or divisible; on the contrary, it is one and most simple, and comprehends all things in one simple act. But as this most simple will of God is employed about a variety of objects, we are obliged, in accommodation to our weak capacities, to recur to distinctions which exist not in the will itself, but in the objects of volition. It is therefore an objective and not a subjective distinction, which we have already stated. I said that the distinction was scriptural. This appears from the fact that both decrees and precepts are called the will of God. Thus the precept is called God's will in Psalm cxliii. 10: "Teach me to do Thy will"—that is, to obey Thy precept. The decree is called God's will in Rom. ix. 19: "Who hath resisted His will?"—that is, Who has frustrated His decree? "Though the precept," says Turrettin, "may fall under the decree, as to the propo-

sition or prescribing of it, yet it does not fall under it as to
the fulfilment or execution"—that is, to give or prescribe
the precept is a part of God's decree, but to secure obedience
forms no necessary part of it at all. "Hence," continues
Turrettin, "the distinction is a just one—the decretive will
being that which determines the certainty of events; and the
preceptive will, that which simply prescribes duty to men.
If this distinction be just, God may, without contradiction,
be said to *will* preceptively, or in the way of command, what
He does not will decretively, or purpose to effect." "Thus
it was His preceptive will that Pharaoh should let the Israelites go, that Abraham should sacrifice his son, and that
Peter should not deny Christ;" but yet none of these things
were decreed. It was not the efficient purpose of God to
cause them be done, as is plain from the event. Yet we are
not to suppose that there is any contrariety in these wills, if
I may so speak. They are different, being employed about
different objects, but are not therefore contrary.

God cannot be said without absurdity to will and not will
the same thing in the same sense; but God may be said to
command a thing which He does not decree shall be done.
He decrees to give the command and to prescribe the rule
of duty, but He does not decree to give or secure obedience.
There is no contradiction here. God commanded Abraham
to offer up his son Isaac: this is God's preceptive will. He
wills to give this precept as a trial of Abraham's faith. But
God decreed that Isaac should not be offered up, as the event
manifestly proved: this is God's decretive will. Is there
any contradiction between them? Is there any inconsistency
in supposing that God should *will* to try Abraham's faith by
such a command, and yet *will* at the same time that Isaac
should not be slain? I would just remark, in concluding
this point, that the preceptive will is the sole rule of duty to
man, as its name shows; and fearful guilt is always incurred
when the commands of God are disregarded or despised. It
is not my business to inquire whether God has a secret decree—that I shall or shall not, in point of fact, comply with

His injunctions; it is enough that I am bound to do so, and am justly held punishable if I do not obey. Whatever rule of operations He may prescribe to Himself, the one which He has given to me is plain and intelligible, and His unrevealed purposes will afford me no shelter if I neglect or disregard it.

Another important truth, which is necessary in this discussion, is, that man is now just as much under the authority of God as he was previously to his fall. He is just as much the subject of command and law as ever he was, and is consequently as much bound to render perfect and entire obedience to all the Divine precepts. It would be preposterous to suppose that his own wilful sin had cancelled moral obligation. If, then, God still continues to be man's rightful sovereign, and man God's lawful subject, if the Lord still possesses the power to command, and man is still under obligation to obey, it should not be thought strange that God deals with man according to this relation, and actually enjoins upon him an obedience to law which He has no determinate purpose to give. This can be regarded as nothing more than the rightful exercise of lawful authority on the part of God; and to deny that He can consistently do this without giving man the necessary grace to obey, is just flatly to deny that God is a sovereign or that man is a subject.

Let these few preliminary remarks be distinctly borne in mind—(1.) That there are various senses in which love, or similar affections, are attributable to God; (2.) that there is a just, natural and scriptural distinction of the will of God into preceptive and decretive; (3.) that the relation of sovereign and subject still remains unchanged between God and man—and I apprehend that there will be very little difficulty in refuting the Arminian hypothesis, that God actually wills or seriously intends the salvation of all men. The passages to which they most confidently appeal for support may be ranged under two classes: First, those which contain statements of general love or mercy; secondly, those in which they suppose an unlimited purpose of salvation is actually revealed.

In regard to the passages of the first class, it is manifest that where the universal epithets are to be taken in their full latitude—which, however, is not always the case—nothing more can be fairly deduced than God's benevolence, which leads Him to bestow blessings upon all men. There is nothing specific about the character or nature of the blessings, or whenever anything specific is stated it is found to be only the common bounties of Providence that the sacred writer had immediately in view. How preposterous, therefore, from such texts to deduce a purpose of universal salvation, as though God could not send rain upon the wicked and unjust without designing to save them! It is vain to allege that such general goodness is never referred to God's love. The Saviour settles the point in Matthew v. 44, 45. There He commands His disciples to love their enemies, to bless them that curse them, to do good to them that hate them, etc. Why? "That ye may be the children of your Father which is in heaven; for He maketh His sun to rise on the evil and on the good, and sendeth rain on the just and on the unjust." Here the disciples are commanded to *love* their enemies, that they might be *like* God. But how does it appear that God loves His enemies? "He maketh His sun to rise on the evil and on the good, and sendeth rain on the just and on the unjust;" in other words, from the *common bounties of Providence*. With such a plain illustration of the fact that God can be said to love without intending to save, it is amazing that such passages as the following should ever have been adduced to prove a purpose of universal salvation: "The Lord is good to all, and His tender mercies are over all His works." I would as soon think of appealing to Romans ix. 22, because God is there said to have endured the vessels of wrath fitted to destruction with much long-suffering.

The second class of passages will be found to involve no more difficulty than the first. We shall consider the most forcible, or those to which Arminians most frequently appeal. The first which I shall notice is found in 2 Peter iii. 9 : "Not willing that any should perish, but that all should come to repentance." I think it exceedingly doubtful whether the words *any* and *all* have an indiscriminate application in this passage. The context would seem to confine them within the limits of the "us" spoken of just above. This will appear by taking the whole verse in its connection : "The Lord is not slack concerning His promise"—that is, the promise of His second coming—"as some men count slackness, but is long-suffering to usward." To whom? We cannot refer the "us" to any but those who in the eighth verse are addressed as "*beloved.*" It would seem, then, to designate only God's elect. Now, why is God long-suffering to His elect? Because He is "not willing that any"—that is, any *of them*—"should perish," but that all—that is, *all of them*—"should come to repentance." In other words, Christ delays His second coming, and will continue to delay it, until all His elect are savingly gathered into His kingdom and His mystical body completed. This, I confess, appears to me to be the most natural and obvious interpretation of the passage. It certainly is grammatical, and harmonizes well with the context. I am aware that Calvin and other respectable writers have given a different interpretation. They make the latter clause epexegetical of the first, and resolve the willingness of God into His precept. The force of the passage in this view would be, "God has commanded men everywhere to repent." This interpretation does no violence to the words of the passage, for they will certainly bear this meaning, but it seems to me to violate the grammatical connection. The next passage occurs in 1 Timothy ii. 4 : "Who will have all men to be saved and to come unto the knowledge of the truth." It is difficult to conceive how this passage can be supposed to prove a purpose of universal salvation. It expresses simply the inseparable connection between salvation and the knowledge of the truth, together with the solemn fact that God enjoins it upon all to receive the truth. It is manifestly God's preceptive will as revealed in the offers and invitations of the Gospel which is here meant; there is not a syllable about any purpose or decree to save all men. Notice the expression: it is, "*who will have;*" it expresses what God is willing or commands that *men should do*, not what he *intends to do Himself.* If the latter had been the meaning, the passage would be, "who *will save* all men," not "who will *have* all men to be saved." The simple distinction of the will of God into preceptive and decretive divests this passage of all its difficulty.

The next which I shall notice is Ezek. xxxiii. 11: "As I live, saith the Lord God, I have no pleasure in the death of the wicked, but that the wicked turn from his ways and live; turn ye, turn ye, from your evil ways, for why will ye die, O house of Israel?" The remarks of Turrettin on this passage are so just and appropriate that I cannot forbear to translate them: "Although God here protests that He has no pleasure in the death of the wicked, but rather that the wicked should turn from his ways and live, it does not follow that God willed or intended, upon any condition, the conversion and life of each and every man. For, besides that conversion cannot be conditional, it being the condition of life itself, it is certain that the prophet is here speaking of God's preceptive and not His decretive will. The word חָפֵץ, which is here used, always denotes complacency or delight. The passage then simply teaches that God is pleased with, or approves, the conversion and life of the sinner, as a thing in itself grateful to Him and suited to His merciful nature. God is pleased with this rather than the death of the sinner, and therefore enjoins it as a duty that men be converted if they expect to be saved. But although God takes no delight in the death of the sinner, considered merely as the destruction of the creature, it does not follow that He does not will and intend it as an exercise of His own justice and as an occasion of manifesting His glory. A pious magistrate takes no delight in the death of the guilty, but still he justly decrees the punishment demanded by the laws. The interrogatory, 'Why will ye die?', is added because God would show to them in these words how death was to be avoided, and that they, by voluntary impenitence, were the sole authors of their own ruin."

The passages, however, which are most confidently relied on as teaching a purpose of universal salvation are those which relate to the atonement of Christ, and which seem to give it an unlimited extent. It is freely admitted that the doctrine of election falls to the ground if an universal atonement—that is, a full *satisfaction* to law and justice for all the sins of every individual—can be fairly demonstrated. There are multiplied passages of Scripture in which the atonement is confined to the elect. Christ, the Good Shepherd, lays down His life only for the sheep. The song of the redeemed in glory seems to proceed upon no other supposition but that of a limited redemption: "Thou wast slain and hast redeemed us unto God by thy blood, *out of* every kindred, and tongue, and people, and nation." The general current of Scripture appears to represent the incarnation and death of the Redeemer as the grand means by which the great purpose of electing love was gloriously accomplished. Hence we are said to be "chosen in Christ." The texts which are supposed to favour the doctrine of universal atonement admit an explanation which does no violence to the laws of language or the analogy of faith. Many of the passages adduced to prove an unlimited design to save each and every individual prove nothing more than an universal offer. No one doubts that the Gospel offer is indiscriminate and general, but this only supposes an all-sufficiency in Christ, without at all implying that Christ actually *intends* to save all to whom the Gospel is preached. The universal epithets in other passages must be restricted by the immediate connection or scope of the passage. Having made these preliminary remarks, I proceed to examine the most prominent passages. 1 Tim. ii. 6: "Who gave Himself a ransom for all, to be testified in due time." The common and familiar application of the word *gave* to the Gospel offer sufficiently determines the meaning of this passage. It teaches only that Christ is offered to the whole world as an abundant and all-sufficient Saviour. The word *testified*, which has a manifest allusion to the proclamation of the Gospel or the public and indiscriminate exhibition of Christ as the Saviour of sinners, who in " due time" should be preached to "every creature," seems to me to confirm this interpretation. Not a word does this passage then contain about the *design* of Christ to satisfy for the sins of each and every individual. 1 John ii. 2 : " He is the propitiation for our sins, and not for ours only, but also for the sins of the whole world." A reference to Romans iii. 25 explains sufficiently the meaning of John : " Whom *God* hath set forth to be a propitiation," etc. That is, Christ is held up to the acceptance of sinners indiscriminately as the only medium of reconciliation with God. He is " set forth," placed before them as " the way, the truth, and the life." Here then is nothing but the indiscriminate offer again. Hebrews ii. 9 : " That He by the grace of God should taste death for every man." The phrase here is limited by the context. In the next verse they are called " many sons," whom Christ intended to bring to glory; and in the eleventh verse they are spoken of as one with Him, and therefore " He is not ashamed to call them brethren." " Every man," therefore, must mean each of these " many sons and brethren," of whose salvation Christ is " the Captain." Such a limitation of the word *every* is common in the Scriptures; compare Gen. vii. 21, Luke iv. 37, Psalms cxix. 101 ; Prov. vii. 12. In all these passages —and multitudes of others might be mentioned—the word *every* is limited by the context or the necessity of the case. In Romans v. 18, Christ and Adam are spoken of as *covenant heads*. The Apostle is establishing the principle of imputation, and illustrates our justification on account of Christ's merits by our condemnation on account of Adam's sin. The principle in both cases was the same—they were both federal representatives. The "all men," then, in one case means all who were represented by Adam in the covenant of works; in the other, all who were represented by Christ in the covenant of grace. The same may be said of 1 Cor. xv. 22.

The next passage may be found in 2 Cor. v. 14, 15 : "For the love of Christ constraineth us; because we thus judge that if one died for all, then were all dead; and that He died for all, that they which live should not henceforth live unto themselves, but unto Him which died for them and rose again." To a candid mind this passage can present no serious difficulty. Two facts are stated which serve mutually to explain and interpret each other—1. Christ died for "all." 2. The "all" for whom He died do not "henceforth live unto themselves, but unto Him which died for them and rose again." The result or end of Christ's death, as stated in the last verse, actually determines the meaning of the "all" in the fourteenth. Even Doddridge, one of the most cautious and timid interpreters of contested passages, has given substantially this interpretation in his paraphrase upon these verses : "For the love of Christ, so illustriously displayed in that redemption He hath wrought, constraineth us; it bears us away like a strong and resistless torrent, while we thus judge, and in our calmest and most rational moments draw it as a certain consequence, from the important principles which we assuredly know to be true, that if one, even Christ, died for the redemption and salvation of *all who should sincerely believe in Him and obey Him*, then were all dead. And now we know that He died for all, that they who live only in consequence of His dying love should not henceforth from this remarkable period and end of their lives, whatever they have formerly done, live to themselves, but that they should all agree that they will live to the honour, glory and interest of Him who died for them, and when He rose again from the dead retained the same affection for them, and is continually improving His recovered life for their security and happiness." I have quoted this long paraphrase merely to show the mutual connection and dependence of the different parts of the passage, which require that the universal epithet should necessarily be limited.[1]

The nineteenth verse of this same chapter is frequently pressed into the service of an unlimited atonement, but by a dreadful distortion of its real meaning. " God was in Christ reconciling the world unto Himself, not imputing their trespasses unto them, and hath committed unto us the word of reconciliation." Two circumstances in the context show that the Apostle is here speaking only of the Gospel offer, or the grant of Christ to sinners indefinitely as an all-sufficient Saviour. The phrase, " God was in Christ," etc., means that God, *for the sake of Christ*, is willing to pardon all who appropriate the Saviour's merits. In other words, all who come to God in Christ—that is, by receiving Jesus as their mediator and intercessor—will find God a reconciled Father. This is the substance of the Gospel offer. Now, that this is the meaning of the Apostle appears plainly from the connection of this verse with the preceding, in which it is said that God " hath given to us the *ministry of reconciliation*—to wit, that God was in Christ," etc. The ministry of reconciliation, then, or the mere preaching of the Gospel, or the offer of salvation in and through Christ, is the Apostle's own explanation of the passage in question. This appears still more evident from the latter part of the nineteenth verse itself: " And hath committed unto us the *word of reconciliation.*" Hence the Apostle in the twentieth verse presses the Gospel invitation. The whole difficulty of the passage will disappear by simply recollecting that God is never a God in Christ to any but a believing sinner. To apprehend Him as a God in Christ is to apprehend Him by saving faith in the merits of His Son. Hence God in Christ, reconciling the world unto Himself, can mean noth-

---

[1] [NOTE BY EDITOR.—In the discussion on the Necessity and Nature of Christianity immediately preceding the present, there may be found (pp. 87, 91) a fuller explanation by the author of this passage.]

ing but God urging it upon sinners to believe. This passage, therefore, lends no support whatever to the dogma of universal atonement. It states only the universality of the external call of the Word, and the solemn duty of sinners to obey it.

The next and last passage which I shall consider is John iii. 16: "For God so loved the world that He gave His only-begotten Son, that whosoever believeth in Him should not perish, but have eternal life." The idea which our Saviour here intended to convey is, that the indefinite offer of salvation in the Gospel is a testimony to the whole world of God's amazing love or grace. The offer of Christ and salvation in Him is often expressed by words which convey the general idea of an unconditional gift or grant.[1] "My Father *giveth* you the true bread from heaven"—that is, sets before you and invites you to partake. "I will also *give* Thee for a light to the Gentiles, that thou mayest be my salvation unto the ends of the earth." "I will *give* Thee for a covenant of the people." Both of these passages seem to refer to the universal publication of the Gospel. The offer of Christ is called a *gift*, because it conveys to sinners a fair, revealed right to receive and rest upon Him for all the purposes of salvation. Such an offer of a Saviour is a standing testimony to the whole world of God's unmerited grace. But there is not a word in this passage about a purpose or decree to save all indefinitely. On the contrary, the limitation of salvation in the close of the verse to believers only is a striking proof that God did not intend to save all. That the giving spoken of in the verse relates only to the Gospel offer is manifest from its being held out as the ground and warrant of faith; the object of the gift is, "that whosoever *believeth* should not perish, but have eternal life." Now, as saving faith receives Christ "*as He*

---

[1] [NOTE BY EDITOR.—Dr. Thornwell, in after life, expressly condemned the view of the "Marrow men," that God the Father makes a "grant" of Christ as by a "deed of gift" to all men. Justice to him, therefore, might warrant the excision of this sentence.]

is offered" in the Gospel, it is manifest that this gift and the Gospel offer must be the same.

The examination which has just been made of the favourite texts of the Arminian writers is sufficient, it is believed, to refute the. dogma that God has any purpose, either conditional or unconditional, of saving all men indiscriminately. There is no revelation of any such intention in the Bible, so that it becomes frivolous and absurd to oppose election with any arguments whatever derived from this source.

The next point in the objection is, that if God has no purpose of salvation toward all men, the invitations of the Gospel become only a mockery. God cannot possibly be sincere in the indiscriminate offer of salvation if He does not intend to bestow it upon each and every individual. This specious objection proceeds upon a gratuitous assumption that the external call of the Word conveys to every sinner to whom it is directed a specific intimation that God designs his own salvation in particular. But this is far from the truth. The Gospel offer is not an expression of *God's* purposes or decrees, but a plain and intelligible ground of duty to *man*. It comes to no one and says, " You individually and particularly are included in God's purpose of saving mercy." If this were the nature of it, none could pretend to reconcile its acknowledged universality with the doctrines of election and reprobation. But this is so far from being the case that it simply gives to sinners a *right* to believe ; it gives them an adequate foundation, a warrantable ground for the exercise of faith. In other words, it is such a general, indefinite, unconditional grant of Christ in all His plenitude of grace as conveys to each and every sinner who hears the joyful sound an unquestionable right to appropriate and apply the Saviour in all His fullness to his own individual case without presumption or blasphemy. God, in the Gospel, holds up a Saviour in all respects suited to the fallen condition of man, and abundantly able to heal the diseases and relieve the miseries of every son and daughter of Adam. The Divine nature of the adorable Redeemer

stamps an *infinite value* upon His doings and sufferings, so
that there can be no possible limitation of the all-sufficiency
of Christ. Holding up this Saviour to sinners in the outward dispensation of the Gospel, God conveys to all indiscriminately a plain right to appropriate Christ for all the
purposes of salvation, and at the same time solemnly assures
men that all who do appropriate Him shall infallibly be
saved. From all this the general object of the Gospel
offer is sufficiently obvious : it is to afford a *lawful ground*
for *faith*. Saving faith is measured by the offer of Christ
in the Gospel, and no man could possibly be required to
believe if he had no lawful right to believe. The command
of God is positive that all men should believe ; the Gospel
offer comes in as a handmaid to the command, and gives all
men adequate authority for believing. Now, in all this
God may be perfectly sincere, while He has no purpose of
actual salvation for all. He is sincere in giving the sinner
a warrant to believe on Christ, and God may certainly give
such a warrant without giving the sinner a disposition to
make use of it. God is sincere in all the promises of the
Gospel, because He will assuredly fulfil them to all who
scripturally embrace them—that is, embrace them as yea
and amen in Christ, the great Trustee of the Covenant, for
no promise is made separate and apart from Him. God is
sincere in His invitations and entreaties, because He is only
urging the sinner to the faithful discharge of solemn and
imperative duty. And surely God as a Sovereign may
require of man and urge upon him the performance of duty
without duplicity or deceit, and yet withhold that strength
which man has basely forfeited, and is now guilty for need-
ing. If God gave sinners a right to believe on Christ, and
then by creating a positive inability should debar them from
believing, the Gospel offer would clearly be a mockery.
But this is not the case. God makes no man an unbeliever.
He commands and urges it upon *all to believe*, and *debars*
none from an access to the throne of grace. They wickedly
debar themselves, and the decree of reprobation leaves them

to walk in the sight of their own eyes and the pride of their own hearts. The Gospel offer, combined with the positive command of God, renders the duty of believing imperative upon all, and therefore leaves every unbeliever utterly without excuse in the sight of God. An all-sufficient Saviour has been held up before him, abundantly able to save all that were ever invited to come; a door of access has been opened to the throne of grace, so that he might have gone with boldness and sought for the mercy which he needed, with the certain prospect of obtaining it. His duty was plainly declared and solemnly enforced, and God put forth no influence upon him to hold him from Christ, had he felt a disposition to go. He is therefore without excuse. But yet the doctrine of reprobation remains unaffected. God withheld grace which He was under no obligation to bestow, and left the sinner to perish in his sins. He opened the eyes of others to see the Saviour in His glory, and to read their own right to receive and appropriate Him in the record of the Word. Thus is election equally unaffected by the nature and design of the Gospel offer.

Let it be borne in mind that the external call of the Gospel simply points out a ground of duty, and all difficulty is removed. This call merely represents God as a sovereign Legislator and man a dependent subject—a truth with which the doctrines of election and reprobation by no means interfere. This external call says not a syllable about the purposes of God in giving or withholding the grace of faith. But when the call is proclaimed among men indefinitely, then comes in election and persuades some to receive and obey it, while others are left utterly without excuse for refusing to do what they had a plain and unquestionable right to do, and were moreover solemnly bound to do.

Secondly. The next leading class of objections to the sovereignty of God comprehends those which are derived from the moral agency of man. They may be reduced to the following heads: 1. Election is inconsistent with liberty, and consequently with accountability. 2. It destroys all solicitude about personal holiness. 3. It renders the means of grace entirely nugatory. These, I believe, are the most prominent; at least, they are more frequently reiterated than any others of this class. I will answer them in order.

1. Election is inconsistent with the moral agency and accountability of man. It will be remembered that this is one of the objections which the Apostle Paul notices in the ninth of Romans: "Thou wilt then say unto me, Why doth He yet find fault? for who hath resisted His will?" Ver. 19.

That the decrees of God do render events absolutely certain is beyond all doubt, but that they change the nature of second causes can never be made out. All that is necessary to constitute moral agency is to be a rational, intelligent being; to possess the faculties and affections which invariably belong to spirit, and without which it would cease to be spirit. Now, election or Divine sovereignty, in its fullest extent, does not destroy the spiritual or intelligent nature of man, and consequently does not destroy what alone is essential to moral agency. Again, the decree of God does not force men to act contrary to their wills. They are conscious of pursuing the bent of their own thoughts and of prosecuting their own plans. No man is dragged or reluctantly driven by the purpose of God into a course of conduct which he does not choose to pursue. How then does the Divine decree make man a mere machine? It is wholly a gratuitous assumption that the *nature* of second causes is at all changed by the purposes of God. Events are certain, the concurrence of causes in producing them is certain; these things are determined, they *must* take place, there is no possibility of failure, but man still continues to be man notwithstanding the decree.

In relation to the reprobate it is constantly denied by Calvinists that God puts forth a positive agency in creating their sinfulness. He does not make them sinners. He does not infuse into their hearts that moral turpitude and carnal enmity from which their actual rebellion proceeds. He ordains their actions as natural events by decreeing to permit them, or by positively appointing them, but He does not originate the sinner's malignity and desperate aversion to holiness. He finds them in the decree of reprobation under the curse of a righteous law, and determines to leave them in their ruin and depravity. He finds them sinners and He leaves them sinners, with the settled purpose of inflicting upon them the merited penalty of death. Where is there any violence offered to their wills? There is manifestly none. They have all the freedom which their corruption and depravity will permit them to possess. They walk in the " sight of their own eyes." " They kindle a fire and walk in the light of their own sparks." They love sin, and freely indulge in it because they love it.

In reference to the elect, it is freely admitted that God by a positive and direct influence is the author of every holy affection in their hearts. It is freely admitted that they are passive in effectual calling until being quickened by His grace they are enabled and inclined to answer the call. But still it is denied that any violence whatever is offered to their wills. This will appear by considering the separate elements of effectual calling. (1.) " The minds of the elect are enlightened spiritually and savingly to understand the things of God." But surely the infusion of light into the soul does not destroy its nature, does not make that a slave which was free before. A new discernment of things does not affect the accountability of man which grows necessarily out of his relations to God. There is no reason why spiritual knowledge, any more than natural knowledge, should affect man's moral agency considered in its own intrinsic nature. Light in no sense can alter the spiritual constitution of the subject enlightened. How preposterous, then, the idea that because man has spiritual light he ceases to be a moral agent!

(2.) The next element of effectual calling is, " taking away their heart of stone, and giving them a heart of flesh." This sentiment in Scripture is variously expressed, but the influence which the Holy Spirit here puts forth is a *creating* influence. A new heart is *created*. Holy susceptibilities are originated which did not exist before. But surely creation involves no contradiction to moral agency, otherwise no created being could be a moral agent. If the mere fact of creation destroyed moral agency, it would be impossible for God to make a moral agent. Besides, the new heart does not change the *essence* of the soul.

(3.) The third element is "renewing their wills, and by His Almighty power determining them to that which is good." Nor is man's liberty at all infringed in this. Previously to the operations of the Spirit man *could* will nothing but sin ; but his will is now renewed by an Almighty power, and determined to that which is good. Does the fact that man is inclined to good by a power which he has *no disposition* to resist prove that he is not an accountable and moral being? If man were reluctantly driven to the choice of good, he would cease to act freely—that is, in conformity with existing dispositions ; but when man delights in what is good, no matter from what cause this delight may have originated, he acts freely in choosing it.

(4.) The last element is, "effectually drawing them to Jesus Christ, yet so as they come most freely, being made willing by His grace." To this no objection can be raised, as it flatly asserts man's freeness and willingness in receiving Christ. I apprehend that the cause of difficulty with many lies in an oversight of the fact that man is passive in regeneration, though active in believing. He is the *subject* of a Divine influence ; and therefore it is no more reasonable to suppose that his *essential* constitution is changed by being acted upon by God than in any other case of external influence. It is true that the influence which God puts forth is efficient ; it secures the intended result, but it is just as true that man acts freely and spontaneously, since the result intended was to determine the will to good. Previously to the operations of the Spirit, the man was *dead ;* he could perform no spiritual action at all. God infuses into him spiritual life. Now this implies ·no violence. In conse-

quence of this life being infused into his soul, he now freely
chooses and embraces that which is good. And here there
is no violence. Where, then, is the inconsistency between
Divine influence and moral agency?

There is a sense in which moral agency is attributed to
man which, I freely confess, is irreconcilable with election.
It consists in making man's will the sole originating cause
of his actions, without any regard to existing dispositions or
extraneous influences. The theory is, that the will can and
does determine itself; that the only reason why man adopts
one mode of action and not another is that his will, in consequence of its own inherent power, so determined itself.
There is no such thing on this scheme as choice, deliberation,
disposition ; the will is arbitrary and sovereign, and submits
to no influence out of itself. To this theory there are insuperable objections: 1st. It makes man wholly independent
of God. The Supreme Being has no more control over the
actions of His creatures, according to this system, than if He
did not exist. The only dependence which they can feel
upon Him is simply for *preservation*. 2dly. It is inconsistent with accountability. As well might a weather-cock
be held responsible for its lawless motions as a being whose
arbitrary, uncontrollable will is his only law. What can
the man account for? His actions have arisen from no
moral considerations whatever ; he acted because he acted ;
and this is the only account he can give. 3dly. It makes
man the author of his own spiritual renovation. Divine
grace, on this scheme, is not efficient; it does nothing.
Everything depends upon the sinner's arbitrary will. God
may expostulate, and warn, and send His Spirit to operate
on the heart, but all in vain unless the sinner's will should
determine itself to Christ and salvation ; in other words,
unless the sinner should convert himself. These are a specimen of the difficulties involved in this absurd theory of
moral agency, which strictly implies only that man is not a
fit subject for a government of laws.

The Scriptures are explicit in stating the unconditional

decrees of God in connection with the responsibility and moral agency of men. There was a plain decree in regard to the death and sufferings of the Lord Jesus Christ, and yet under that decree the agency of man was exerted in deeds of darkness. So far was this decree from annulling human responsibility that fearful guilt was incurred by the Jews, and tremendous sufferings inflicted upon them. "Him, being delivered by the determinate counsel and foreknowledge of God, ye have taken, and by wicked hands have crucified and slain." Acts ii. 23. "For, of a truth, against Thy holy child Jesus, whom Thou hast anointed, both Herod and Pontius Pilate, with the Gentiles and people of Israel, were gathered together for to do whatsoever Thy hand and Thy counsel determined before to be done." Acts iv. 27, 28. Now here it is expressly said that the enemies of our Lord acted only "according to the determinate counsel and foreknowledge of God," and did only what His "hand and His counsel determined before to be done," and yet they are charged with guilt and wickedness: "ye have taken, and by *wicked* hands have crucified and slain." Hence, the Apostle was clearly of opinion that the absolute and sovereign predestination of God did not take away responsibility from man or remove the guilt of his transgressions. All the difficulties involved in the doctrine, or that have ever been charged upon it, are involved in, and with equal propriety may be charged upon, this particular case. Election to grace is no stronger a feature of the absolute predestination of God than the death and sufferings of Christ; and if all the circumstances connected with the one could be positively decreed and rendered absolutely certain, consistently with the liberty of moral and rational agents, then all the circumstances connected with the other may also be determined without the destruction or infringement of the agency of man.

If efficient Divine influence is inconsistent with moral agency, then men can never be confirmed in holiness beyond the grave without ceasing to be moral agents. God cannot secure their holiness in heaven consistently with their liberty, any more than He can determine their actions here. The difficulty grows out of the sinner's own mind—his own liberty of moral action ; and so long as that liberty continues, the same difficulty must continue. Upon the Arminian hypothesis, then, it is a possible, if not a probable, case, that a soul may have basked for myriads and myriads of years in the rays of eternal glory, and then fall, and fall like Lucifer, never to rise again—suddenly exchanging its shouts of praise and alleluia for the wail of the damned, and dropping the song of redeeming love for the gnashing of teeth and the fiend-like yell of despair. These monstrous results necessarily grow out of the position that election and moral agency are incompatible, and carry along with them so complete a denial of many promises of Scripture as at once to over-throw the fundamental position on which they depend. What then ? We are compelled to receive election with its inevitable concomitant, moral necessity, or resort to wild and revolting theories of free-will with their cumbrous train of absurdity and nonsense. We are compelled to receive a moral agency which is consistent with a moral necessity, or adopt a hypothesis which destroys accountability at once. I cannot forbear to mention here that the difficulty presses just as hard in another form against the Arminians. They deny the Divine decrees, but admit the essential omnis-cience of God. Events, therefore, are certain ; they must happen just as God knows that they will happen ; they can-not possibly happen otherwise. Here, then, is a moral neces-sity just as strong as the moral necessity of the Calvinists. But they reply that God does not *produce* the events. It is a question of no manner of importance how the events are pro-duced ; the difficulty lies in this, that they are *necessarily* pro-duced. Arminians cannot evade it ; their system involves moral necessity as much as ours ; and it is as much their business as ours to reconcile this necessity with moral agency.

2. The next objection of this class is that election destroys all solicitude about personal holiness. It reduces men to a

system of such stern necessity that there is no reason at all why they should be concerned about their personal salvation. It will be seen that this difficulty grows out of the former. I shall make but two or three remarks upon it— (1.) As the nature of second causes is not at all changed by the Divine decree, the duties of man to God are just the same that they would be if there were no election in the case. Man's relations to his Maker are the same; he is still a creature and a subject. The connection of obedience and life is.the same, and all the motives to activity and diligence remain unchanged. With none of these things do the decrees of God interfere. How then can election destroy solicitude about personal salvation? It cannot justly do it without destroying the inseparable connection between holiness and happiness, and the duty of man to obey his sovereign. Exhortations are useful and proper, because man *ought* to obey, and will be abundantly rewarded if he does. (2.) It would contradict the very nature and design of election if it made men careless and indifferent. The end contemplated by election is holiness. The decree is that the chosen ones shall believe, repent, be humble and exemplary in their walk and conversation, and yet this has a tendency to make them stupid, unconcerned and indifferent! Because it is decreed that a man shall believe, *therefore* he will *not* believe; because it is decreed that he shall be *holy, therefore* he will be profligate and abandoned. What absurdity! So long as holiness continues to be an indispensable element of salvation, the election to grace cannot be an election to sin. Election as much involves the certainty of personal holiness as it does the certainty of heaven. (3.) My third remark is, that it has directly a contrary tendency, and that in several respects. It is an acknowledged principle of human nature that when great interests are at stake deep solicitude is felt by men, if there is only a bare possibility that they may be personally concerned. If the means of knowing whether or not they are in fact concerned be within their power, they will resort to them with eager avidity.

This is a plain principle of human nature. Apply this to the case in hand. Here are solemn and commanding interests at stake. Heaven or hell will infallibly be the lot of every child of Adam. Here are the means of knowing, in the inspired volume, with certainty whether I am predestinated to eternal life. If I really *believed* all this, I would shake heaven and earth in the great commotion; I would give no sleep to my eyes nor slumber to my eyelids till I had settled this solemn point. Just let me realize the *certainty* that heaven or hell is my portion, and I could no more fold my arms under the bare possibility of going to hell, while there was a prospect of escape, than I could take my ease on a burning volcano. The certainty of *one* doom, but the uncertainty in regard to *which*, has a natural tendency to rouse the soul into vigorous efforts to throw off the pangs of suspense.

If the Scriptures pointed out by name and surname the individuals elected and reprobated, there would be some foundation for the objection, but they do no such thing. They simply tell men that they belong to one class or the other, and add as an encouragement to effort that those who comply with the prescribed plan of salvation are certainly elected. Hence they call upon us to make our "calling and election sure" by receiving the Saviour and walking in the way of His commandments. None know that they are reprobates, and therefore none can know that their efforts will be useless. I am fully satisfied that if men had a deeper and more impressive sense of the truth of this doctrine, there would be more earnest inquiry and serious alarm among the careless and impenitent. But the misfortune is that they do not *feel* the astounding certainty that heaven or hell is theirs. They are radically Arminians; they have the keys of both kingdoms in the pocket of their own free-will, and rest satisfied under the full but delusive impression that *they* can determine the matter just when they please.

In reference to those who know that they are elected, it cannot be maintained that election has a tendency to lull them into carnal security, unless it is also maintained that a deep and clear sense of God's love to us has a tendency to call forth only hatred to Him. This would be to make a Christian not only depraved, but unnatural in consequence of conversion. The biography of the saints furnishes a running commentary upon the happy moral influence of Calvinism in quickening and invigorating the graces of the Spirit, and some Arminians have been candid enough to confess that the charge of licentiousness is the offspring of ignorance. It is obvious, in fact, that there are some graces of the Christian character which a cordial belief of election is wonderfully suited to cherish.

(1.) " We love Him because He first loved us." " Without the doctrine of predestination," says Zanchius, " we cannot enjoy a lively sight and experience of God's special love and mercy towards us in Christ Jesus. Blessings not peculiar, but conferred indiscriminately on every man without distinction or exception, would neither be a proof of peculiar love in the donor, nor calculated to excite peculiar wonder and gratitude in the receiver. For instance, rain from heaven, though an invaluable benefit, is not considered as an argument of God's special and peculiar favour to some individuals above others, because it falls on all alike, as much on the rude wilderness and the barren rock as on the cultivated garden and fruitful field. But the blessing of election, somewhat like the Sibylline books, rises in value proportionably to the fewness of its objects. From a sense of God's peculiar, eternal and unchangeable love to His people their hearts are inflamed to love Him in return. Slender indeed will be my motives to the love of God on the supposition that my love to *Him* is beforehand with *His* to me, and that the very continuance of His favour is suspended on the weather-cock of my variable will, or on the flimsy thread of my imperfect affection. Such a precarious, dependent love were unworthy of God, and fitted to produce but scanty and cold reciprocation of love from man. Would you know what it is to love God as your Father,

Friend and Saviour, you must fall down before His electing mercy. Till then you are only hovering about in quest of true felicity. But you will never find the door, much less can you enter into rest, till you are enabled to love Him because He hath first loved you." It is manifest that a doctrine so friendly to the love of God cannot be unfriendly to universal obedience, "for love is the fulfilling of the Law." The man who sincerely loves God, as a matter of course, will desire conformity to His image, and as " electing goodness is the very life and soul of love to God, good works must flourish or decline in proportion as election is glorified or obscured."

(2.) This doctrine is peculiarly favourable to the cultivation of humility, and that in two respects. 1st. It lays the axe at the root of all human merit, and ascribes to sovereign, unmerited grace the whole glory of our salvation. It is found from experience that the legality of the heart presents a formidable barrier to the reception of the Gospel. Men's performances are so essential to their own self-complacency that it is hard to persuade them that all their righteousnesses are as filthy rags, and that salvation is not the reward of debt, but the gift of grace. This very natural pride of the carnal heart can be humbled or removed by no truth so effectually as the doctrine of election. When this is brought home upon their minds, men can then understand that " it is not of him that willeth, nor of him that runneth, but of God that showeth mercy." It strips them of all pretensions to merit, shows them their deep and loathsome unworthiness, and prostrates their souls in the very dust of self-abasement. The following remarks of Zanchius are forcible and appropriate : " Conversion and salvation must, in the very nature of the things, be wrought and effected either by ourselves alone, or by ourselves and God together, or solely by God Himself. Pelagians were for the first, the Arminians are for the second, true believers are for the last, because the last hypothesis, and that only, is built on the strongest evidence of reason, Scripture, and experience. It most effectually hides pride from man, and sets the crown of undivided praise upon the head—or, rather, casts it at the feet—of that glorious Triune God 'who worketh all in all.' But this is a crown which no sinners ever yet cast before the throne of God who were not first led into the transporting views of His gracious decree to save freely, and of His own will, the people of His eternal love." 2dly. This doctrine is not only favourable to humility by counteracting a legal spirit, but it is the very soul of dependence on Divine influence. The importance which the Scriptures attach to an uniform, habitual dependence on the grace of God sufficiently appears from the frequent and earnest exhortations to cultivate such a disposition; and if indeed it be so that the Holy Spirit is the source of all pious and devout affections, this dependent temper is the only one which is consistent with a Christian's true condition or his relations to God. Emptied as we are by election of all that cannot abide the scrutiny of heaven, we are pointed to inexhaustible treasures at God's right hand, which are bestowed only upon those who habitually depend upon His grace. Blind, naked and miserable in ourselves, we take the counsel of the Holy Spirit and lean upon the Lord for all that we need. Self-annihilation, as Luther calls it, is the mainspring of uniform dependence upon grace; and whatever has a tendency to drive us out of ourselves has likewise a tendency to drive us to God.

(3.) The doctrine of election affords great encouragement to prayer. 1st. Because prayer is the natural expression of dependence upon Divine influences. 2dly. Because election represents the grace of God as efficient. There would be no motive to pray for spiritual blessings if our growth in grace depended upon our own free wills and not upon the Spirit of God. If Divine grace exerted no invincible efficacy in subduing sin, mortifying lust and invigorating the principles of piety, it would be hard to determine why the life of a Christian should be a life of habitual, unceasing prayer. 3dly. Election is favourable to prayer, because it represents it as a *gift* of God, and as the appointed medium of receiving Divine blessings. When God decrees to bestow a blessing upon His people, He decrees also to give them the Spirit of prayer and supplication, so that when they find this Spirit poured out upon them they have every encouragement from the usual order of Divine providence to "ask in faith, nothing doubting."

(4.) This doctrine is the sole foundation of a full assurance of faith. It is the duty and privilege of Christians not only to be assured of their present acceptance with God, but also of their future, everlasting salvation. But this assurance they never could possess if justification, sanctification and glorification were not inseparably connected in the Divine decree. That such an assurance is in the highest degree friendly to piety is manifest from the fact that faith itself, even in its lowest exercises, works by love and purifies the heart.

Such are some of the obvious tendencies of election. I have said nothing of the support which it yields in affliction and distress, the patience and submission with which it inspires the soul in the gloomiest hours of adversity, and the strong consolation it administers to the dying saint when struggling in the pangs of death. Enough has been said, however, to show that its tendencies are all in favour of godliness, and I regard it as no proof of the spirituality of the present age that amid our bustle and excitement so little is said of this precious doctrine of the Gospel.

That wicked and profane persons have perverted it to their own eternal undoing I have no disposition to deny. So has every doctrine of the Gospel been perverted. The difficulty is not in the doctrine, but in the heart; swine will trample on a jewel be it ever so precious.

3. The last objection under this head is that election renders the means of grace perfectly nugatory. If the elect are to be saved they will be saved, let them do what they will; if the reprobate are to be damned they will be damned, let them do what they may. This objection involves a contradiction. Salvation implies faith, and repentance, and

holiness, and it is perfect nonsense to say that men may believe and repent let them be as skeptical and profligate as they may. Faith necessarily supposes the *Word*, which is the only ground of faith, and the Word is usually dispensed by preaching, and hence the indispensable necessity of an instituted ministry. God's decrees are accomplished through the medium of second causes, and the means of grace are the appointed channels through which He dispenses the blessings of the Gospel. They are a necessary part of the decree. When God determines to save He determines to send His Word and ordinances, and to render them efficacious by the mighty operation of His Spirit. There is no inconsistency in this. God decrees to send rain upon the earth, but He first collects the vapours into clouds. A caviller might say, if it is to rain it will rain, whether there be any clouds or not.

The means of grace in themselves have no efficiency. They cannot convert a single soul; all their efficacy is derived from God and from His electing grace. They are valuable only because He has decreed them as the medium of His blessings. But yet it would seem as if the objectors supposed that the means of grace possess in themselves an inherent efficacy, for how else can election be opposed to them? I shall conclude this head with two extracts from Zanchius: "They who are predestinated to life are likewise predestinated to all those means which are indispensably necessary in order to their meetness for entrance upon and enjoyment of that life, such as repentance, faith, sanctification and perseverance in these to the end. Now, though faith and holiness are not represented as the cause wherefore the elect are saved, yet these are constantly represented as the means through which they are saved, or as the appointed way wherein God leads His elect to glory, these blessings being always bestowed previously to that. Agreeable to all which is that of Austin: 'Whatsoever persons are, through the riches of Divine grace, exempted from the original sentence of condemnation are undoubtedly brought *to hear the Gospel,* and when heard, they are caused to believe.'" The next extract is more to the point: "That absolute predestination does not set aside nor render superfluous the use of preaching, exhortation, etc., we prove from the examples of Christ Himself and His apostles, who all taught and insisted upon the article of predestination, and yet took every opportunity of preaching to sinners, and enforced their ministry with proper rebukes, invitations and exhortations as occasion required. Though they showed unanswerably that salvation is the free gift of God and lies entirely at His sovereign disposal, that men can of themselves do nothing spiritually good, and that it is God who of His own pleasure works in them both to will and to do, yet they did not neglect to address their auditors as being possessed of reason and conscience, nor omit to remind them of their duties as such. Our Saviour Himself expressly and *in terminis* assures us that no man *can* come to Him except the Father draw him, and yet He says, Come unto me, all ye that labour. St. Paul declares it is not of him that willeth nor of him that runneth, and yet exhorts the Corinthians so to run as to obtain the prize. He assures us that we know not what to pray for as we ought, and yet directs us to pray without ceasing. St. James, in like manner, says that every good and perfect gift cometh down from above, and exhorts those who want wisdom to ask it of God. So, then, all these being means whereby the elect are frequently enlightened into the knowledge of Christ, and by which they are, after they have believed through grace, built up in Him, and being means of their perseverance in grace to the end, they are so far from being vain and insignificant that they are highly useful and necessary, and answer many valuable and important ends without in the least shaking the doctrine of predestination in particular or the analogy of faith in general."

We have now given what was promised at the outset: 1. A plain statement of the doctrine of Election as held by the Presbyterian Church. 2. A vindication of its truth by an appeal to the Scriptures. And, 3. We have answered, as we hope satisfactorily, the leading and prominent objections of those who are opposed to Calvinism. The Essay must now stand or fall by its own merits. If it maintains the doctrines of the Bible, it is a comfort to think that God will take care of His own truth, whatever may become of this feeble effort to defend it; if the doctrines here advanced are false, the sooner they fall to the ground the better. Nothing now remains to complete our design but the deduction of a few obvious inferences.

1. This doctrine pre-eminently glorifies God, and that in several respects. (1.) It glorifies the independence and omnipotence of the Divine will. Every other scheme renders the plans and purposes of God in some measure dependent upon the conduct and determinations of his creatures, and Arminians have no hesitation in avowing that the designs of God are susceptible of failure, although He solemnly declares, "My counsel shall stand, and I will do all my pleasure." It is the will of God, we are told, that each and every man should be saved. The fact that all are not, and will not be, saved, shows one of two things—either that God *could not* accomplish His own design, or that the Divine will is dependent on the will of the creature. Hence God either has no settled purpose of His own, or is unable to carry it out as He would wish. This is the necessary and unavoidable consequence of conditional decrees; they virtually dethrone God by making the volitions of man of equal importance in the government of the world with His own. They destroy at once His independence and omnipotence. But the doctrine of predestination ascribes to God that which unquestionably belongs to Him, the supreme disposal of all events "according to the counsel of His own will." "Our God is in the heavens, He hath done whatsoever He hath pleased. There is none that can stay His hand or say unto him, What doest Thou?" Creation and Providence are nothing but the actual evolutions in time of the secret purpose which lay in the bosom of God from

all eternity. There is nothing fortuitous, nothing accidental, nothing unexpected, because nothing does or can take place which has not been previously determined by "the counsel and foreknowledge of God." While God as yet existed alone, supremely glorious in Himself, before one particle of matter had been called into being or a solitary soul was found to adore and reverence the perfection of Deity, He scanned in the light of an infallible omniscience and fixed by the power of an immutable decree all objects and events, whether small or great, whether grand or minute. He simply *wills*, and emptiness and desolation become peopled with a thousand inhabitants of a thousand ranks and gradations of being, the wheels of Providence begin to roll, and every creature, whether small or great, organic or inorganic, material or intelligent, walks in the track which an eternal purpose had settled and arranged. "According, therefore, to the Scripture representation," says Toplady, "Providence neither acts vaguely and *at random*, like a blind archer who shoots uncertainly in the dark as well as he can, nor yet *pro re nata*, or as the unforeseen exigence of affairs may require; like some blundering statesman who plunges, it may be, his country and himself into difficulties, and then is forced to unravel his cobweb and reverse his plan of operations as the best remedy for those disasters which the court-spider had not the wisdom to foresee. But shall we say this of God? 'Twere blasphemy! He that dwelleth in the heavens laugheth all these miserable afterthoughts to scorn. God who can neither be overreached nor overpowered has all these post-expedients in derision. He is incapable of mistake. He knows no levity of will. He cannot be surprised with any unforeseen inconveniences. 'His throne is in heaven, and His kingdom ruleth over all.' Whatever, therefore, comes to pass, comes to pass as a part of the original plan, and is the offspring of that prolific series of causes and effects which owes its birth to the ordaining and permissive will of Him in whom 'we all live, and move, and have our being.'

Providence in time is the hand that delivers God's purpose of those beings and events with which that purpose was pregnant from everlasting." All events hang upon the nod of Jehovah, while His purposes and plans are dependent upon nothing but the "unsearchable counsel of His own will." He is the mighty Ruler of the universe, and His *will, His eternal purpose*, is supreme and irresistible through all the boundless ranges of existence. Amid the seeming irregularity and confusion which distract the world, amid all the failures in human schemes and calculations which are daily taking place, amid the horrors of war, the fall of kingdoms and the ruins of empire, there is one grand, unchangeable purpose which never fails, but which meets its accomplishment alike in the frustration or success of all other purposes. Every event in nature or in grace is simply an evolution of that grand purpose; and could the thread of this purpose be traced by the limited intellect of man in all its bearings and relations, chaos would exhibit regularity, and order and harmony would rise from confusion. In fact, the *glory* of the Divine independence and omnipotence is so inseparably connected with predestination that even Unitarians when describing the Divine majesty forget their system and substantially acknowledge the fundamental principles of Calvinism. They cannot portray the majesty of God without it. Hence the following extract from Buckminster's Sermon on Providence need not surprise us: "How inexpressibly great is that Being who penetrates at once the recesses and circumscribes within Himself the boundless ranges of Creation; who pierces into the profound meditations of the most sublime intelligence above with the same ease that He discerns the wayward projects of the child; who knows equally the abortive imaginations and the wisest plans of every creature that ever has thought or ever will think throughout the realms of intellect! How wonderful is that power which wields with equal ease the mightiest and the feeblest agents, directs the resistless thunder-bolt, or wafts a feather through the air; bursts out in the im-

Vol. II.—13

prisoned lava, or rests on the peaceful bosom of the lake; rides on the rapid whirlwind, or whispers in the evening air! Think, I pray you, of that wisdom which conducts at the same moment the innumerable purposes of all His creatures, and whose own grand purpose is equally accomplished by the failure or success of all the plans of all His creatures. Think of Him under whom all agents operate, because by Him all beings exist. Think of Him who has but to will it, and all moving Nature pauses in her course, chaos succeeds to the harmony of innumerable spheres and eternal darkness overwhelms this universe of light. Yet in the midst of darkness His throne is stable and all is light about the seat of God!" It is really amazing that any one who has correct apprehensions of the moral character of God should be at all opposed to the supremacy and independence of His righteous will. Supremely just, and wise, and holy, it ought to be a matter of thanksgiving and joy that such a Being controls the armies of heaven and the hosts of earth, and all should join the shout of the redeemed in glory, "Hallelujah, the Lord God Omnipotent reigneth!"

(2.) This doctrine not only glorifies the omnipotence and independence of God's will, but furnishes an illustrious display of His grace. The Scriptures represent the grace and mercy of God as the only sources from which all our blessings are derived, and particularly the saving blessings of the Gospel. We are everywhere described in the Bible as having no claim upon God, but as being justly exposed to His wrath and curse. Polluted and defiled by nature, we are under a righteous sentence of condemnation, and all holy beings would approve the severity of the Divine judgment, if we, like the devils, were eternally cut off from all hope of pardon or acceptance. This is the natural state of every soul of man, and this is the light in which God saw us when the purpose of salvation went forth in favour of His elect. He saw them in their *blood*, and when nothing could have been justly expected but vengeance and death, He said unto them, " *Live*." Here was *grace*—pure, unmerited favour—breaking through all the barriers of their depravity and guilt, and yearning toward them with an amazing purpose of redemption and life. But the questions might well have been asked, "How shall I put thee among the children?" "How shall I reconcile the conflicting claims of grace and justice and prepare my elect for an inheritance among them that are holy?" Here *grace* becomes still more wonderful. It pitches upon the eternal Son, the second person of the adorable Trinity, and enters into a solemn covenant transaction with Him to redeem, and sanctify, and save. He undertakes, as the Substitute and Surety of the elect, in the fullness of time to become their kinsman by being born of a woman; to humble Himself by being found in fashion as a man; to obey the law as a covenant in their name, and to bring in an everlasting righteousness; to redeem them from its awful curse by being made a curse for them; and to satisfy completely in their behalf all the claims of justice and of law, so that God consistently with His adorable perfections could regard them with an eye of favour and acceptance. The next step in this glorious economy of grace is the mission of the Holy Spirit to apply the purchased redemption to the hearts of the elect by His efficient, almighty operations. Here, then, is an astonishing display of grace, such as can consist with no other doctrine but that of election. Here is a chain of Divine love reaching from the great decree of salvation in the counsels of eternity to its full accomplishment in the regions of glory. Not one link of this golden chain hangs upon human merit—all, all from first to last is pure, unmerited grace. No wonder that the Apostle, in speaking of election, breaks forth into doxologies, for that doctrine erects an eternal monument to the glory of God's grace. It brings down every lofty imagination, abases every high thought that exalts itself against God, and issues forth the solemn and peremptory edict that "no flesh shall glory in His presence." "But of Him are ye in Christ Jesus who of God is made unto us wisdom, and righteousness, and sanctification, and redemption, that according as it is written, he that glorieth let him glory in the Lord." "Blessed be the God and Father of our Lord Jesus Christ, who hath blessed us with all spiritual blessings in heavenly places in Christ Jesus, according as He hath chosen us in Him before the foundation of the world, to the *praise of the glory of His grace*, wherein He hath made us accepted in the Beloved." This grace becomes remarkably conspicuous, because it is confined to the elect. Such a limitation of its objects shows in the light of undeniable reality its utter undeservedness. Had it been promiscuously extended to all, its freeness could not have been so remarkably displayed, but by being withheld from some the demerit of all is unanswerably established, and just in proportion as that is established the freeness of Divine grace is exalted. It is a flimsy cavil that grace to be infinite must include every possible object; then, verily, the devils would be saved. The plain truth is that the Divine attributes are all infinite only as they exist in God, and not in relation to the number or extent of the objects on which they are exercised.

(3.) This doctrine glorifies God's justice. " But what if God, willing to show His wrath and to make His power known, endured with much long-suffering the vessels of wrath fitted to destruction?" Romans ix. 22. "The two objects," says Professor Hodge, "which Paul here specifies as designed to be answered by the punishment of the wicked, are the manifestation of the wrath of God and the exhibition of His power. The word *wrath* is used here as in chapter i. 18, for the Divine displeasure against sin, the calm and holy disapprobation of evil, joined with the determination to punish those who commit it. Though the inherent ill desert of sin must ever be regarded as the primary ground of the infliction of punishment—a ground which would remain in full force were no beneficial results anticipated from the misery of the wicked—yet God has so ordered His government that the evils which sinners incur shall result in the manifestation of His character, and the consequent promotion of the holiness and happiness of His intelligent creatures throughout eternity." I would only add that if sin be an infinite evil, the Divine displeasure against it must be signal and conspicuous ; but if God had included the whole human race in His gracious purpose of salvation, it might be a question whether mercy had not eclipsed justice. But by graciously electing some and passing by others the Divine justice is doubly manifested : First, in the sufferings and death of Christ as the Substitute of the elect ; and, secondly, in the persons of the reprobate themselves. But be this as it may, the punishment of the wicked can never be regarded as otherwise than just ; and so long as God continues to be supremely holy and opposed to sin, it cannot be thought strange that the terrors of His wrath should overtake the guilty.

I have now shown, in these few and simple observations, that the doctrine of Election glorifies God, particularly His independence, omnipotence, grace and justice. But I do not mean to insinuate that God elected one and rejected another for the purpose of merely displaying His character. This is the natural and obvious result, but it by no means follows that this was the cause. On the contrary, it is the plain and undeniable doctrine of the Scriptures that " His counsels are unsearchable, and His ways past finding out." The reasons of the Divine procedure are the secret things which are known only to Himself. We know facts, and in many cases we can trace results ; but we " know not the mind of the Lord," and cannot, without arrogance and presumption, undertake to inquire into the why and the wherefore of the Divine administration. He simply declares that He " worketh all things according to the counsel of His own will." This is all that He has revealed, and it is all that we are able to ascertain. When we reach the will of God we must stop ; we can go no farther. Why He wills so and so is a question which we are utterly unable to solve, and it is darkening counsel by words without knowledge when we presume to prate about the general good of the universe and the greatest happiness of the greatest number. No doubt God has reasons for the conduct of His government, but we know them not; His *will* is law to us and the utmost boundary of our knowledge. Manifestly, the efficient cause of election and reprobation, in the Scriptures, is referred only to the sovereign will of Jehovah, as has been proved already at considerable length. But we should by no means confound this with the final cause or natural result which is certainly the manifestation of His glory; or, as the Confession of Faith expresses it, election is "to the praise of His glorious grace," and reprobation "to the praise of His glorious justice." By observing this necessary distinction between efficient and final causes we shall sail clear of the dangerous quicksands of Hopkinsian error.

2. The second inference which I would deduce from this doctrine is the infallible perseverance of the saints. This results necessarily from the immutability of God. His counsel shall stand—His will cannot be defeated, and therefore all the objects of His special love must necessarily be saved. The certainty of election is the ground of Paul's triumphant assurance in the eighth of Romans: "Who shall separate us from the love of Christ? Shall tribulation, or distress, or persecution, or famine, or nakedness, or peril, or sword? Nay, in all these things we are more than conquerors through Him that loved us. For I am persuaded that neither death, nor life, nor angels, nor principalities, nor powers, nor things present, nor things to come, nor height, nor depth, nor any other creature, shall be able to separate us from the love of God which is in Christ Jesus our Lord."

3. The next inference which may safely be drawn is the doctrine of limited atonement. We have seen that God has no purpose of salvation to all—that He has no design whatever of saving the whole human race; and, therefore, it is preposterous to suppose that the satisfaction of His Son was specifically intended for each and every individual. No doubt it is sufficient, because, in consequence of the union of

the two natures in the person of Christ, His sufferings possess an *infinite* value. No one denies the abundant sufficiency of Christ's merits to save this world and ten thousand others; but the question is, whether or not the satisfaction of the Saviour was designed for any but His own elect—whether it was rendered in the name of any others, or was intended to be available to their salvation? Now, if the doctrine of election and reprobation be true, such an unlimited design would appear to be impossible. How can God intend to save those toward whom He has no purpose of salvation? The two doctrines are wholly irreconcilable,—if election and reprobation be true, universal atonement must fall to the ground; if universal atonement be true, then election must be blotted from the pages of the Bible. As a matter of course, I speak of the work of Christ in the light of a *satisfaction* to Divine justice—the only light in which it is regarded in the word of God. As to that refined system of error which makes the atonement of Christ nothing but a pompous pageant, to amaze and astonish a gazing universe, this is not the place to refute its vapouring pretensions. It is at best a mere creature of the fancy, and entitled to no more respect than the mad ravings of a sick man's dream. Now, if the atonement of Christ is a strict satisfaction to the law and justice of God, in the name and place of every sinner, it is impossible to conceive how God, without manifest injustice, can pass any by and doom them to punishment in their own proper persons. They have already satisfied the law in the person of Christ. How can they then be possibly condemned? Does justice require two satisfactions? We may safely say, then, that universal atonement is not only inconsistent with the doctrine of election, but absolutely incompatible with the ultimate damnation of a single sinner; it is, in other words, when legitimately carried out, nothing but the plain, unvarnished doctrine of universal salvation. It is not necessary, in order to give a warrant of faith and to render it the duty of every sinner to believe on Christ. The offer of the Saviour in the Gospel, which has no reference on its face to the secret designs of God, is the only legitimate ground of faith, and the command of God would render it binding upon every soul to believe on the Saviour, even though He had died for only one solitary sinner. The right of men to receive and rest upon Christ depends not upon the unrevealed purposes of God in regard to His death, but upon the broad and un-limited grant which is contained in the Gospel record, with its cheering invitations and pressing injunctions. In other words, faith fastens on the preceptive and not the decretive will of God. It would certainly imply a defect of some sort in the economy of grace to suppose that Christ died indis-criminately for all men; that is, with the specific design of saving each and every individual, when, in point of fact, it is generally conceded that all men will not be saved. It is much more honourable to the Divine character to limit the design to the number that will actually be redeemed, and to maintain with the advocates of this scheme that the all-sufficiency of the atonement is an adequate ground of a general offer, and the sovereign authority of God an ade-quate ground of a general obligation to believe.

I have now completed my original design. It is unneces-sary to say that consequences of momentous importance, in-volving the fundamental principles of the Gospel, hang upon the reception or rejection of this doctrine. To the humble Christian, who has been taught it by the Spirit of God—who has been emptied of self in every form and shape, and brought in deep prostration of soul to bow at the footstool of sovereign mercy—it is inexpressibly precious; and he knows something of the spirit in which that song, so often in his mouth, was dictated : " Not unto us, O Lord, not unto us, but unto Thy Name give the glory." In this precious doctrine he finds constant food for humility, gratitude and love; and when tempted to flag in his Christian course, nothing affords a stronger stimulant to duty than a deep sense of God's eternal, unmerited grace—" Lo, I have loved thee with an everlasting love." This doctrine is emphatically children's bread. They are often supported by the nourishment it contains, and strengthened for the race set before them, when they can give no connected, metaphysical account of their experiences or feelings. It is eminently devotional in its tendencies; and it is to be regretted that we are so often compelled to chastise the feelings which it naturally excites, in order to enter the lists of cold-blood argument with those who would rob us of this jewel which our Master has given us. We are often compelled to *reason* when the heart would prompt us to *adore*. It is a scriptural duty to *contend*, and contend *earnestly*, for the faith once delivered to the saints. " Now, unto the King, eternal, immortal, invisible, the only wise God, be honour and glory for ever and ever. AMEN."

www.ingramcontent.com/pod-product-compliance
Lightning Source LLC
LaVergne TN
LVHW021610080426
835510LV00019B/2505